transformed by *Praise*

transformed by Praise

The Purpose and Message of the Psalms

MARK D. FUTATO

P&R
PUBLISHING
P.O. BOX 817 • PHILLIPSBURG • NEW JERSEY 08865-0817

Italics in Scripture quotations indicate emphasis added.

Page design by Tobias Design
Typesetting by Michelle Feaster

Printed in the United States of America

Library of Congress Cataloging-in-Publication Data

Futato, Mark David.
Transformed by praise : the purpose and message of the Psalms / Mark D. Futato.
p. cm.
Includes bibliographical references and index.
ISBN 0-87552-190-8 (pbk.)
1. Bible. O.T. Psalms—Criticism, interpretation, etc. 2. Spiritual life—Christianity. I. Title.

BS1430.52 .F88 2002
223'.206—dc21

2001055457

To my wife,

Adele,

with whom I have experienced

God's transforming grace.

PSALM 128

A song for the ascent to Jerusalem.

How happy are those who fear the LORD—
all who follow his ways!
You will enjoy the fruit of your labor.
How happy you will be! How rich your life!
Your wife will be like a fruitful vine,
flourishing within your home.
And look at all those children!
There they sit around your table
as vigorous and healthy as young olive trees.
That is the LORD's reward
for those who fear him.
May the LORD continually bless you from Zion.
May you see Jerusalem prosper as long as you live.
May you live to enjoy your grandchildren.
And may Israel have quietness and peace.

(New Living Translation)

Contents

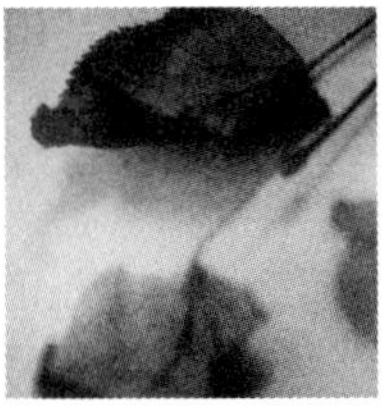

PREFACE

Just as a caterpillar is transformed into a beautiful butterfly, God is in the process of transforming our lives into something ever more beautiful day by day. God uses many tools in bringing about this transformation. One tool he has used in my life and in the lives of thousands of people is the Book of Psalms. *Transformed by Praise: The Purpose and Message of the Psalms* tells the story of the power of the Psalms to change your life.

I have been studying and teaching the Book of Psalms for years. *Transformed by Praise* is the fruit of some of that work. The chapters in this book started out as lectures delivered to students at Reformed Theological Seminary in Orlando, Florida. I gave these lectures at the culmination of several years of great turmoil and transformation in my own life and in the life of my family. God changed my life in that process of teaching others about the transforming power of the Psalms, and I am delighted to bring this teaching to you in the hope that you, too, will experience more of the life-changing grace that God has for you in the Book of Psalms.

Along with the Psalms, God uses people in the process of

changing our lives. God has used my wife, Adele, more than anyone else, as an agent of change in my life. We have lived the Psalms together, experiencing their agony and their ecstasy. Adele's keen understanding of life has at many points deepened my understanding of the Psalms. Her unseen hand is present throughout this book. Adele is the fruitful and flourishing vine spoken of by the ancient psalmist (Ps. 128:3).

Many thanks go to Jan Bubaker, my assistant at RTS, who transcribed the lectures for me. Her help in other ways made my work all the more pleasant.

I am grateful to Allan Fisher at P&R Publishing for his willingness to accept my manuscript for publication and to Linda Triemstra and Thom Notaro, whose editing skills transformed the manuscript into a finished product. The staff at P&R has been a delight to work with.

We are all in process. We are all becoming more of what God created us to be. May the Spirit of the risen Lord transform you through *Transformed by Praise*.

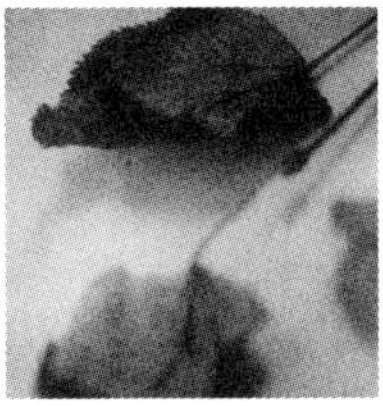

1

PRAISE THE LORD

The Psalms as Praise

Praise the LORD.

Praise God in his sanctuary;
praise him in his mighty heavens.
Praise him for his acts of power;
praise him for his surpassing greatness.
Praise him with the sounding of the trumpet,
praise him with the harp and lyre,
praise him with tambourine and dancing,
praise him with the strings and flute,
praise him with the clash of cymbals,
praise him with resounding cymbals.

Let everything that has breath praise the LORD.

Praise the LORD. (Ps. 150)

Praise is the dominant note in this final song of the Book of Psalms. Every line calls us to praise the Lord. Thirteen times we are invited to praise him. He is to be praised on earth and in heaven. We are to praise him for his actions and his attributes. We are to praise him with an orchestra of instruments. And every living creature is to join the chorus.

Praise is the dominant note not only in this final song but also of the Book of Psalms as a whole. The praise of God is a golden thread that runs through the fabric of the book. And the vocabulary of praise is rich. In Hebrew there are three basic words for the praise of God. One we translate "praise," one we translate "bless," and one we translate "give thanks." There are other words as well, like "exalt," "extol," and "glorify." Then there are all sorts of related words for singing to the Lord, making music to the Lord, shouting to the Lord, and clapping to the Lord. Praise is the dominant note of the Book of Psalms.

And as we will discover, praise is the dominant note of our lives. We have all known to one degree or another times of ecstasy when our hearts overflowed with praise for God—for who he is and for what he has done in our lives. Such praise is to characterize our lives this side of heaven.

But praise is not the only note sounded in the book, because praise is not the only note that has been heard in our lives. In January 1997 without any warning my family became seriously ill. The symptoms of uncontrolled muscle spasms were first seen in our daughter, the youngest of four children. Before long the whole family was experiencing these spasms. There were nights when the spasms I experienced were severe enough to awaken my wife from a sound sleep. Then my wife's health collapsed. We know what it means to walk through the valley of the shadow of death.

Through those difficult days God has transformed my understanding of the abundant life to which he calls us. The Lord provided me with a number of sources for that transformation. One key source was my wife. I benefited greatly from the transforming grace she experienced. A second source was the Book of Psalms. While we were walking through the valley of the shadow of death, I was writing a commentary on the Book of Psalms. My wife and I often marveled at how a particular psalm I was studying matched so well what we were experiencing at the time. The Psalms were my lifeline to God in days of doubts and fears and soul-searching questions.

The Lord has turned our wailing into dancing and removed our sackcloth and clothed us with joy that our hearts might not be silent and that we might give him praise (Ps. 30:11–12). Let's experience together more of God's abundant life as we probe the depths and heights of the invitation of the Book of Psalms to praise the Lord.

PRAISE IS THE MESSAGE OF THE TITLE

A key insight into the Book of Psalms is found in the ancient Hebrew title. The message found in the ancient title can be summarized in one word: praise. We could call the Psalms the Book of Praises.

The Book of Praises

There are two different ancient titles for the Book of Psalms. One comes from the Hebrew tradition. The other is from the Greek and Latin traditions.

The Title in Hebrew. The title of the Book of Psalms in Hebrew is *sayfer tehilleam*, or *tehilleam.*[1] Translations into English would be "book of praises" or "praises." This particular Hebrew word for "praises" is unique; it is used nowhere else except in the title of this book. The related verb is used frequently in the Book of Psalms and is translated "praise."

One interesting note is that only one psalm in the book has the word *praise* in the ancient title, and that is Psalm 145, "a psalm of praise." So why did the ancient Hebrews call this book of poems the Book of Praises?

Even more interestingly, of the two major kinds of the psalms—happy psalms and sad psalms, or psalms of praise and psalms of lamentation—there are more psalms of lamentation than there are psalms of praise. If we were going to name the Book of Psalms based on the statistically most frequent kind of psalm, we would call it the Book of Lamentations. So again we ask, Why the ancient title Book of Praises?

Before we answer that question, let's discover where the title Book of Psalms comes from.

The Title in English. The English title comes from the ancient Latin tradition, which called the book *Liber Psalmorum*, or Book of Psalms. The Latin title is based on the ancient Greek title, *Biblō Psalmōn*, or Book of Psalms. So in the New Testament we read, for example,

David himself declares in the Book of Psalms [*biblō psalmōn*]:

"The Lord said to my Lord:
'Sit at my right hand
until I make your enemies
a footstool for your feet.' "
(Luke 20:42–43)

Again we read,

"For," said Peter, "it is written in the book of Psalms [*biblō psalmōn*],

'May his place be deserted;
let there be no one to dwell in it,'

and,

'May another take his place of leadership.' "
(Acts 1:20)

The ancient Greeks also used the title *Psalterium*, from which we get our word *psalter*. Although this title is not as common these days, the Book of Psalms is still referred to as the Psalter.

Greek *psalmos* ("psalm") is not a translation of the Hebrew word for "praise." Greek *psalmos* is a translation of the Hebrew word *mizmor*, which is used fifty-seven times in the ancient Hebrew psalm titles and is best translated "psalm" (see, e.g., the titles to Pss. 3–6). Both *psalmos* and *mizmor* mean a song accompanied by stringed instruments. So once again the question arises: Why the ancient title Book of Praises?

Before we answer that question, let's look at the way of praise.

THE WAY OF PRAISE

What does "praise the Lord" mean? The Book of Psalms gives us two answers.

"Praise the Lord" Is an Exclamation

First, "praise the Lord" is an exclamation. In English we typically use the words "praise the Lord" as an exclamation. If someone were to walk up to you and say, "Praise the Lord," would you sense that you were being asked to do anything? If you would have any inclination to do something in response, it would probably be to answer with another "Praise the Lord!" because we typically use the words "praise the Lord" as an exclamation.

"Praise the Lord" is also used in the Book of Psalms as an exclamation. The common expression *hallelujah* is a transliteration into English of a Hebrew expression that we translate "praise the Lord." With one exception (Ps. 135:3), "hallelujah" occurs only at the beginning or the end of a number of psalms (see, e.g., Ps. 112; 150). In these cases "hallelujah" or "praise the Lord" serves as a kind of introductory and concluding exclamation of praise. So "praise the Lord" is an exclamation in the Book of Psalms.

But most of the time when we read the words "praise the Lord," we are not reading an exclamation. We are encountering a command.

"Praise the Lord" Is a Command

If you were to say to someone, "Open the door," and this person were to respond by saying, "Open the door," you would probably think it a little odd. If you were to say to someone, "Open the door," you would expect that person to do something—to open the door.

So it is too in the ancient Hebrew tradition and in the Book of Psalms. When somebody said, "Praise the Lord," this person was looking for a response. "Praise the Lord" is a command like "Open the door." So our question is How do we carry out the command to praise the Lord?

We don't primarily carry it out by saying, "Praise the Lord," although that is one possibility. We carry out the command by acknowledging something. To praise is to acknowledge. Praising God is acknowledging who he is and what he has done. Praising is confessing what God has done in the history of salvation. Praising is confessing what God has done in our lives. We carry out the command to praise the Lord by acknowledging and confessing who God is and what he has done, and in so doing, we render honor and glory to the One who is the object of our praise.

Let's look at a couple of examples of praise in the Bible. The first example is found in Nehemiah 9:5–7. Here the Levites command the people to praise the Lord:

> And the Levites . . . said: "Stand up and praise the LORD your God, who is from everlasting to everlasting."

Then the people carry out the command:

> Blessed be your glorious name, and may it be exalted above all blessing and praise. You alone are the LORD. You made the heavens, even the highest heavens, and all their starry host, the earth and all that is on it, the seas and all that is in them. You give life to everything, and

> the multitudes of heaven worship you. You are the LORD God, who chose Abram and brought him out of Ur of the Chaldeans and named him Abraham.

This is praise: confessing who God is, what he has done—in this case what he has done in creating the universe and in choosing Abraham for a special purpose.

The second example is found in Psalm 103:1–14. In the first two verses the psalmist exhorts himself to praise the Lord:

> Praise the LORD, O my soul;
> all my inmost being, praise his holy name.
> Praise the LORD, O my soul,
> and forget not all his benefits—

The following verses then show us the psalmist carrying out his command by reciting how God typically acts and what qualities characterize God:

> who forgives all your sins
> and heals all your diseases,
> who redeems your life from the pit
> and crowns you with love and compassion,
> who satisfies your desires with good things
> so that your youth is renewed like the eagle's.
> The LORD works righteousness and justice
> for all the oppressed.
>
> He made known his ways to Moses,
> his deeds to the people of Israel:
> The LORD is compassionate and gracious,
> slow to anger, abounding in love.

He will not always accuse,
  nor will he harbor his anger forever;
he does not treat us as our sins deserve
  or repay us according to our iniquities.
For as high as the heavens are above the earth,
  so great is his love for those who fear him;
as far as the east is from the west,
  so far has he removed our transgressions from us.
As a father has compassion on his children,
  so the LORD has compassion on those who fear him;
for he knows how we are formed,
  he remembers that we are dust.

The psalmist praises the Lord by reciting the Lord's actions: he forgives, heals, redeems, crowns, satisfies. The psalmist also recites God's attributes: he is gracious, compassionate, slow to become angry, and abounding in love. This is praise: confessing who God is and what he has done in our lives.

So back to the question, Why the title Book of Praises? Having discovered that praise is the message of the title, we will now find out that praise is also the message of the Book of Psalms.

Praise Is the Message of the Book

In the last fifteen to twenty years there has been a lot of scholarly research on the Book of Psalms, in particular studying whether the individual psalms are in a random order or whether the psalms have been purposefully arranged. While all the evidence is not yet in, there is sufficient evidence to demonstrate that the psalms have been purposefully arranged. At this point in our study we will look at one aspect of this purposeful arrangement. We will look at other aspects of the arrangement of the psalms in later chapters.

The Book of Psalms Moves from Lamentation to Praise

There is clear movement in the overall structure of the Book of Psalms. Again, if we consider two of the main kinds of psalms, psalms of lamentation and psalms of praise, there is movement in the Book of Psalms from lamentation to praise.

The Book of Psalms Begins with Lamentation

Although laments are spread throughout the Book of Psalms, the laments are piled up at the beginning of the book. Let's look at a few examples by reading the opening lines of some of the psalms at the front of the book.

> O Lord, how many are my foes!
>   How many rise up against me!
> Many are saying of me,
>   "God will not deliver him." (Ps. 3:1–2)

> Answer me when I call to you,
>   O my righteous God.
> Give me relief from my distress;
>   be merciful to me and hear my prayer. (Ps. 4:1)

> Give ear to my words, O Lord,
>   consider my sighing. (Ps. 5:1)

> O Lord, do not rebuke me in your anger
>   or discipline me in your wrath.

Be merciful to me, LORD, for I am faint;
  O LORD, heal me, for my bones are in agony.
My soul is in anguish.
  How long, O LORD, how long? (Ps. 6:1–3)

O LORD my God, I take refuge in you;
  save and deliver me from all who pursue me,
or they will tear me like a lion
  and rip me to pieces with no one to rescue me.
    (Ps. 7:1–2)

Why, O LORD, do you stand far off?
  Why do you hide yourself in times of trouble? (Ps. 10:1)

How long, O LORD? Will you forget me forever?
  How long will you hide your face from me?
How long must I wrestle with my thoughts
  and every day have sorrow in my heart?
  How long will my enemy triumph over me?

Look on me and answer, O LORD my God.
  Give light to my eyes, or I will sleep in death;
my enemy will say, "I have overcome him,"
  and my foes will rejoice when I fall. (Ps. 13:1–4)

Do you now have a feel for where the Book of Psalms starts? Not only do you feel how the Book of Psalms starts, but also you have probably felt these same emotions at times in your experience. You too have had times of walking through the valley of the shadow of death. The words of these psalms have perhaps articulated the deep agony of your heart and of your soul. The

Book of Psalms starts on this dominantly negative note of lamentation—of suffering, sorrow, and grief.

But this is not where the Book of Psalms ends. It may start with lamentation, but it ends on a glorious note of praise.

The Book of Psalms Ends with Praise

Just as the laments are piled up at the beginning of the Psalms, a mountain of praise brings the Psalms to a close.

> Praise be to the LORD my Rock,
> who trains my hands for war, my fingers for battle.
> (Ps. 144:1)

> I will exalt you, my God the King;
> I will praise your name for ever and ever.
> Every day I will praise you
> and extol your name for ever and ever.
>
> Great is the LORD and most worthy of praise;
> his greatness no one can fathom.
>
> My mouth will speak in praise of the LORD.
> Let every creature praise his holy name
> for ever and ever. (Ps. 145:1–3, 21)

Then Psalms 146, 147, 148, 149, and 150 begin with "hallelujah/praise the LORD," and all five of these psalms also end with "hallelujah/praise the LORD." The Book of Psalms comes to a climax in Psalm 150, where praise is commanded thirteen times, and where every colon of every line contains the verb *praise*, and where the last line shouts, "Let everything that has breath praise the LORD" just before one final "praise the LORD."

Do you now feel the difference between the beginning of the book and the end? The difference between "How many are my foes, O LORD, how many rise up against me" and the repeated "Praise the LORD"?

It is clear that at least in a general way the psalms have been arranged in a purposeful order. There is movement from the beginning of the book to the end, a movement from songs of lamentation to songs of praise, from the chords of suffering to the chorus of glory.

The Book of Psalms has much to teach us about worship. The overall shape of the book teaches us that our worship is to be doxological. This means that the dominant and perhaps even the final note of our worship is ordinarily to be praise.

Many churches over the years have had the tradition of singing the doxology as the end of the service:

> Praise God from whom all blessings flow.
> Praise him all creatures here below.
> Praise him above ye heavenly host.
> Praise Father, Son, and Holy Ghost.

This is a wonderful tradition, although it is not necessary to sing the doxology or any other particular song at the end of every worship service. But do you see the appropriateness of ending the service on a note of praise, based on the climax of praise in the Book of Psalms? This communicates something fundamental about the orientation of our worship. It communicates, as we will see, something about the fundamental nature of our lives.

The Book of Psalms also teaches us about balance and emphasis in our worship. It teaches us that it is appropriate for our worship to provide us with opportunities to express all of life's experiences: the lamentation and the praise, the negative and the positive. Worship can be a time of honestly bringing to God the doubts and fears and the anxieties and sorrows that may be in our minds and on our hearts. But while it's appropriate in worship to bring to expression that dark side of life (some people have called it "the dark night of the soul"), the dominant note in worship, and even the concluding note in worship, is appropriately a word of praise. As the Book of Psalms moves from lamentation to praise, God is teaching us something in that movement, something about our worship and something about our lives.

Before we look at what this movement teaches us about our lives, let's look at how the psalms of lamentation move from lamentation to praise.

THE PSALMS OF LAMENTATION MOVE FROM LAMENTATION TO PRAISE

Just as there are different kinds of music—jazz, blues, soul—and just as there are different kinds of poetry—limerick, epic, haiku—so there are different kinds of psalms—hymns, laments, thanksgiving. As we have seen, the lament is the most frequent kind of psalm in the book. Laments have a particular structure. That structure can be expressed in the phrase "from plea to praise."

The Lament Begins with the Negative

A lament typically begins on a negative note by rehearsing the trouble that the psalmist is experiencing and pleading with God for deliverance but then ends on a positive note of confidence or praise. Let's look at Psalm 22 as an example.

Psalm 22 begins with that well-known and agonizing cry,

My God, my God, why have you forsaken me?
  Why are you so far from saving me,
  so far from the words of my groaning? (v. 1)

This psalm was written when David was in deep distress, feeling as if he had been abandoned by God. David felt as if God were miles and miles away from him, too far away to save him from his trouble. As we continue reading through the first half of this psalm we get insight into the depths of David's agony:

I am a worm and not a man,
  scorned by men and despised by the people.
All who see me mock me;
  they hurl insults, shaking their heads. (vv. 6–7)

Roaring lions tearing their prey
  open their mouths wide against me.
I am poured out like water,
  and all my bones are out of joint.
My heart has turned to wax;
  it has melted away within me.
My strength is dried up like a potsherd,
  and my tongue sticks to the roof of my mouth;
  you lay me in the dust of death.
Dogs have surrounded me;
  a band of evil men has encircled me,
  they have pierced my hands and my feet.
I can count all my bones;
  people stare and gloat over me.
They divide my garments among them
  and cast lots for my clothing. (vv. 13–18)

These words express the darkness of the days David was experiencing. He was in deep distress and feeling isolated, even from his God:

> Do not be far from me,
> for trouble is near
> and there is no one to help. (v. 11)

The laments typically begin with this kind of negative speech. But then something extraordinary takes place in these dark psalms.

An Extraordinary Shift in Mood

As the Book of Psalms shifts from lamentation to praise, so do the laments themselves. There is a radical turn in these psalms from the deeply negative to the remarkably positive.

In Psalm 22 this turnaround takes place at verse 22. The mood reverses from "My God, my God, why have you forsaken me?" to "I will declare your name to my brothers; in the congregation I will praise you." David's words have turned from lamentation to praise.

In keeping with this reversal, we read in the latter half of the psalm,

> You who fear the LORD, praise him!
> All you descendants of Jacob, honor him!
> Revere him, all you descendants of Israel! (v. 23)

> From you comes the theme of my praise in the great assembly;
> before those who fear you will I fulfill my vows.

The poor will eat and be satisfied;
  they who seek the LORD will praise him—
  may your hearts live forever! (vv. 25–26)

Psalm 22 may be a dramatic example of this shift in mood, but it is by no means a unique example. This shift is characteristic of the laments. The question is How do we explain this shift? How can someone be in the valley of the shadow of death one moment and on the mountaintop one verse later?

We don't know for sure. But here are some possibilities.

Perhaps articulating the darkness brought relief. We can experience cleansing by honestly articulating the deep pain in our souls. Holding on to the pain and grief and perplexity and pretending that we have it all together when we don't will not bring the relief we are looking for. Some level of relief can come, however, when we honestly go before God and tell him exactly what we think and how we feel. Have you ever done this? Have you ever honestly told God how you feel and what you are thinking? I mean honestly? Through the laments the Holy Spirit invites us, encourages us, to pray with this kind of utter honesty.

Have you ever prayed with such honesty? You are free to. One reason you can be so honest with God is that he already knows how you are feeling and what you are thinking. You don't need to worry about coming to God with complete honesty. He knows the depths of your pain and perplexity when your soul is lost in the darkness. And I can testify that when you can't see him, when you can't feel him, when you doubt that he's there, he is—and his arms are open wide, as he says, "Come, tell me what you think and what you feel." He can handle your doubts and fears and perplexing questions just as well as he handled those of David and others when they prayed the laments recorded in the Book of Psalms. Honest prayer can have a cleansing effect on the soul.

But this inner cleansing is not the total answer, because the psalmists were not simply looking for psychological or spiritual relief. They were looking for solutions to problems in their lives. Another possibility is that after the expression of agony a priest spoke a word that promised relief and enabled faith to rise above the circumstances.

Think of Hannah (1 Sam. 1). Hannah was in deep distress because she was barren and because her rival wife, Peninnah, was constantly tormenting her. The Bible tells us that "in bitterness of soul Hannah wept much and prayed" (1 Sam. 1:10). And her prayer was such an honest expression of her pain that Eli the priest thought she was drunk! Now that's honest praying. But Hannah was not drunk. She was a woman in deep trouble who was pouring out her soul to the Lord in great anguish and grief (1 Sam. 1:15–16). Eli then said to her, "Go in peace, and may the God of Israel grant you what you have asked of him" (1 Sam. 1:17). This word from God through the priest Eli had a transforming effect on Hannah, for the Bible tells us that she "went her way and ate something, and her face was no longer downcast" (1 Sam. 1:18). Then, in 1 Samuel 2, we read a remarkable poem. We read Hannah's song of praise to the God who delivered her from her trouble by empowering her to conceive a child.

In keeping with Hannah's experience, the radical shift that takes place in the laments may be owing to the life-changing power of the Word of God. The Word has the power to give you hope when you have despaired, to bring you faith where your doubts once reigned, to replace the curse with blessing in your life, blessing from the God who hears and answers the cry of your soul.

Another related explanation for the shift in the laments from the negative to the positive is a gap in time. Perhaps the first part of Psalm 22 was written in January and the last part was written in November. And in between God acted in a marvelous and miraculous way to bring about deliverance. This was part of Hannah's experience. Not only did the Word of God transform her soul as soon as she received it, but also in time God acted and gave her the child she so longed for. Then came her song of praise.

Although we cannot explain with certainty how the remarkable shift takes place in the laments, we do know that there is a movement from lamentation to praise in the laments and in the Book of Psalms.

Now we are in a position to see that the Book of Psalms is a portrait of the life of Jesus Christ. It is not just one or two or ten or 150 individual psalms that are messianic, that are about Jesus. The book as a whole is about Jesus, because this movement in the Book of Psalms from lamentation to praise, from suffering to glory is a portrait of the life of Christ.

JESUS' LIFE MOVED FROM LAMENTATION TO PRAISE

Like the laments and the Book of Psalms, Jesus' life moved from lamentation to praise. After his resurrection from the dead, Jesus met two men on the road to Emmaus. Since they had put all of their hope in Jesus and they thought that Jesus was dead, they were in despair. Jesus they told them that if they had only understood the Old Testament, they would have known that he was first to suffer and then to enter his glory (Luke 24:26). Suffering to glory, lamentation to praise is a description of Jesus' life.

Jesus Sang the Laments

While I have known the feeling of being abandoned by God and while David knew the feeling of being abandoned by God, nobody has known the dark night of the soul as Jesus did when he was on the cross. On the cross Jesus sang the psalms of lamentation as no one had ever sung them up to that point, and no one since that time has sung them out of those same depths of agony. On the cross Jesus sang the lament recorded in Psalm 22:

> About the ninth hour Jesus cried out in a loud voice, "*Eloi, Eloi, lama sabachthani?*"—which means, "My God, my God, why have you forsaken me?" (Matt. 27:46)

Though David felt abandoned by God, David had not truly been abandoned. While I have felt abandoned by God, I have never truly been abandoned. But when Jesus felt abandoned on the cross, it was because he was truly abandoned by his heavenly Father. Jesus experienced the agony of ultimate abandonment by God as nobody has ever known it.

And so you have a High Priest who can relate to you no matter where you are because he's not just been where you have been; he's been far beyond the darkest despair in your experience. He understands. And his heart is full of love and compassion and comfort for you. Jesus sang the songs of lamentation when he was on the cross.

Jesus Sings the Song of Praise

In the New Testament not only are the words of Psalm 22:1 found on the lips of Jesus, but so are the words of Psalm 22:22. Hebrews 2:12 records Jesus as saying,

I will declare your name to my brothers;
in the presence of the congregation I will sing your praises.

Jesus too made that remarkable shift from lamentation to praise, from suffering to glory. We know what explains the remarkable shift that Jesus made: his resurrection from the dead. Although we may not be able to fully explain how the modern person or the ancient psalmist makes this transition, the ultimate answer lies in the resurrection of Jesus Christ from the dead. Jesus suffered the agony of hellish separation from the Father and came out victorious on the other side singing the songs of praise. And he does not sing them by himself but sings them "in the presence of the congregation," for he sings not for himself alone but for us as well.

Jesus sang the laments for us. So there is a sense in which we will never have to sing the laments, not in their ultimate depths. We may sing them honestly but never ultimately, never as one truly abandoned by God, because Jesus was abandoned in our place. There is therefore now no abandonment for those who trust in Christ Jesus. Through Christ Jesus the power of the Spirit of life has set us free from the power of sin and death (Rom. 8:1–2).

Jesus also sang the psalms of praise for us and now sings them with us. Because Jesus' life moved from lamentation to praise, our lives move from lamentation to praise as well.

Our Lives Move from Lamentation to Praise

The Book of Psalms is not only Jesus' story; it is also our story. Because it is Jesus' story, it is our story, as we are united to him by faith. The Book of Psalms is our book.

There may be times when we must sing songs of lamentation. Paul tells us in Romans 8:23,

> We ourselves, who have the firstfruits of the Spirit, groan inwardly as we wait eagerly for our adoption as sons, the redemption of our bodies.

We live in a world that is affected by what we could call God's common curse. This is the misery the world has been subjected to because of our rebellion against God. Moses speaks of this misery in Genesis 3:17–19, and Paul reflects back on it in Romans 8:20.

> For the creation was subjected to frustration, not by its own choice, but by the will of the one who subjected it.

The creation was "subjected to frustration" by God, not because of what it had done but because of what we had done.

> We know that the whole creation has been groaning as in the pains of childbirth right up to the present time. Not only so, but we ourselves, who have the firstfruits of the Spirit, groan inwardly as we wait eagerly for our adoption as sons, the redemption of our bodies. (Rom. 8:22–23)

There may be times when we have to say, "My God, my God, why have you forsaken me?" "How long, O LORD, will you forget me forever?"

But the final song in our lives is not the song of lamentation. The final song is the song of praise. As surely as the Book of

Psalms moves from lamentation to praise, so most assuredly do our lives move from lamentation to praise. This is so because Jesus' life has moved from lamentation to praise for us.

We will be part of that final chorus that hears this call, "Let everything that has breath praise the LORD!" There is no doubt about it. And that's why now the dominant note in our lives is the song of praise.

Doesn't Paul tell us that we are already seated with Christ in heaven? Do you believe that? We are already seated with Christ in heaven, where he is singing the song of praise in the assembly. And his song of praise penetrates back into this life and is the dominant song in our lives.

Paul says, "We ourselves, who have the firstfruits of the Spirit, groan inwardly." It is true that we may groan, but it is also true that we "have the firstfruits of the Holy Spirit." We have the firstfruits of that eternal song of praise in our hearts already. And we are all in the process of experiencing transformation. We are all on a journey. We are all on a pilgrimage. We are all moving from lamentation to praise.

And so, Paul says,

> We, who with unveiled faces all reflect the Lord's glory, are being transformed into his likeness with ever-increasing glory, which comes from the Lord, who is the Spirit. (2 Cor. 3:18)

We have ever-increasing praise in our hearts and on our lips as we more and more become conformed to the image of the Lord Jesus Christ, who has already sung the lament for us and now sings the hymn of praise with us. And how does this transformation come about? It comes "from the Lord, who is the Spirit."

The Spirit of God is within us as the firstfruits of the fullness of praise and doxology. We have all the resources that we need to have praise as the dominant note of our lives.

The apostle Paul says in Ephesians 1:3,

> Praise be to the God and Father of our Lord Jesus Christ, who has blessed us in the heavenly realms with every spiritual blessing in Christ.

And notice, he doesn't say that God has blessed us "with some spiritual blessings," nor does he say, "with many spiritual blessings." He says, "with every spiritual blessing." We have everything that we need in Christ, his Spirit, and his Word. We have everything that we need for life and godliness, now and forevermore.

I don't know what you are experiencing at this time in your life. Maybe you are in the valley of the shadow of death. Maybe you are on a mountaintop of praise. Maybe you are somewhere in between. Maybe you are not even sure where you are. But God knows. And God is at work that you might experience more of his abundant life (Rom. 8:28) for his praise. And this is possible because, in coming to give you abundant life, Jesus has sung the lament for you and now invites you to sing the song of praise with him.

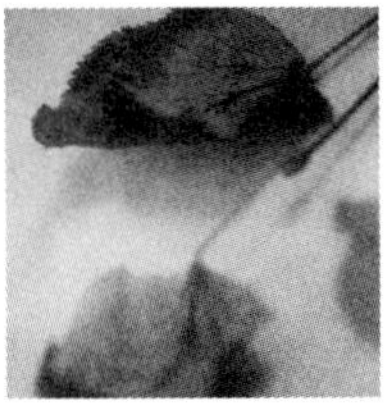

2

Open My Eyes

The Psalms as Poetry

Open my eyes that I may see
wonderful things in your law. (Ps. 119:18)

I have a friend who had his first book of poetry published a few years ago.[1] The type of poetry he writes is called haiku, and here is one of my favorites from this collection:

fog.
sitting here
without the mountains

If you are like me, you do not have a technical understanding of the nature of haiku. But through reading my friend's poetry, I have come to enjoy haiku.

I enjoy listening to the blues. Even without a technical knowledge of the differences between blues and jazz, I still enjoy the blues.

I also enjoy reading the Hebrew poetry found in the Bible. But my enjoyment of Hebrew poetry is deeper than my enjoyment of either haiku or the blues. One of the reasons for this is that I have acquired knowledge of the nature of Hebrew poetry. Hebrew poetry is quite different from English poetry, and understanding how Hebrew poetry works has enriched my understanding and enjoyment of the poetry of the Old Testament.

So I have two goals for you in this chapter. By the time you have finished reading this chapter, I want you to understand the poems of the Bible better—those in the Book of Psalms in particular—and to enjoy them more. Experience has taught me that these two goals go together, because the more you understand the poetry of the Bible the more you will enjoy it. And the more you enjoy it, the more you will read it and grow in your understanding of it.

I opened this chapter with one verse from Psalm 119. This poetic line begins, "Open my eyes that I may see," and after the word *see* there is a pause in the poetry. "See what?" we wonder as we pause. "Wonderful things," says the poet. And where are these wonderful things found? "In your law." In the next chapter we will learn in some detail what the Hebrew word translated "law" means and where we can find this law. But for now let me say that the word means "instruction," and you can find this instruction in the poetry of the Book of Psalms.

The psalmist no doubt has the content of the poetry in mind when he refers to "wonderful things." But since the psalmist was a poet, I wouldn't be surprised if some of the wonderful things that he wanted to see are the wonderful things that are embedded in the aesthetic quality of the poetry. You see, form and meaning work together in poetry. Understanding the poetic form heightens your understanding of the meaning that is embedded in the form. My prayer is that through your reading of this chapter, God will open your eyes to see more of the beauty and more of the meaning of his Word found in the poetry of the Psalms.

Before we launch into the details, let me give you a brief working definition of Hebrew poetry. *Hebrew poetry is a type of literature that uses parallelism and imagery in high frequency.* Since Hebrew prose can contain parallelism and imagery, it is the high frequency of these features—the consistent and sustained use of them—that distinguishes poetry from prose. Other features distinguish Hebrew poetry from prose; there are, for example, Hebrew grammatical features that distinguish the prose account of creation in Genesis 1 from the poetic description of creation found in Psalm 104. But since we are learning to understand and enjoy the poetry of the Psalms in an English translation, it is sufficient for us to focus on parallelism and imagery as the two primary features of Hebrew poetry.

POETRY IN PARTS

Let's begin by discovering the basic parts of a Hebrew poem. Psalm 111 provides us examples of most of these basic parts.

The Colon

A colon is a subunit of a poetic line. In Psalm 111:1 you read, "I will extol the LORD with all my heart." That is a colon. "In the counsel of the upright and in the assembly" is a second colon. Verse 2 begins with a colon, "Great are the works of the LORD," and ends with a colon, "they are pondered by all who delight in them." Each verse can be segmented into cola (the plural of colon, like phenomena is the plural of phenomenon).

The Line

A line is a unit of poetry comprising one or more cola.

Notice that Psalm 111 opens with "praise the LORD." "Praise the LORD" is a poetic line that is made up of only one colon, which we call a *monocolon*. Monocola are not frequent.

Much more frequent is the *bicolon*. In fact, the bicolon is the most frequent type of poetic line in the Old Testament. A bicolon is a poetic line formed with two cola. Verse 1 contains a bicolon: "I will extol the LORD with all my heart" (colon A) and "in the counsel of the upright and in the assembly" (colon B).

Modern translations, like the New International Version, often use a series of indentations to indicate the cola. The first colon (colon A) will be on the left margin. The second colon (colon B) will always be one indentation in. So Psalm 111:1 is laid out as follows:

> I will extol the LORD with all my heart
>   in the council of the upright and in the assembly.

Sometimes there will be a third indentation, and this third indentation means that there wasn't enough room in the column to get the entire colon on one line, so the publisher had to wrap the colon down to the next line.

Verses 2–8 are all bicola:

> Great are the works of the LORD;
>   they are pondered by all who delight in them.
> Glorious and majestic are his deeds,
>   and his righteousness endures forever.
> He has caused his wonders to be remembered;
>   the LORD is gracious and compassionate.
> He provides food for those who fear him;
>   he remembers his covenant forever.
> He has shown his people the power of his works,
>   giving them the lands of other nations.
> The works of his hands are faithful and just;
>   all his precepts are trustworthy.
> They are steadfast for ever and ever,
>   done in faithfulness and uprightness.

More frequent than the monocolon but considerably less frequent than the bicolon is the *tricolon*, a line formed with three cola.

The third colon (colon C) will be indented once, like colon B. Verses 9–10 provide examples of tricola.

> He provided redemption for his people,
> he ordained his covenant forever,
> holy and awesome is his name.
>
> The fear of the LORD is the beginning of wisdom;
> all who follow his precepts have good understanding.
> To him belongs eternal praise.

Thus far we have seen that cola are grouped together into lines usually made from two cola but sometimes made from one or three.

The Strophe

Just as similar cola are grouped together to form a line, similar lines are grouped together to form a strophe. Or, to put it another way, a strophe is a group of lines that are more closely related to each other than they are to the surrounding lines. A strophe is in poetry what a paragraph is in prose.

Modern translations indicate the division between two strophes by placing a blank line between the two. This blank line functions like the indentation that marks the beginning of a new paragraph in English prose. The New International Version divides Psalm 111 into three strophes. Verse 1 is the first strophe. This strophe expresses the psalmist's intention to praise the Lord. The second strophe is made up of verses 2–9 and contains the praise proper, as these verses recount who God is and what he has done. Verse 10 forms the final strophe, which concludes the poem with a wisdom saying. Segmenting a poem into strophes helps us to better understand the flow of the poet's thought and thereby helps us to better understand the poem.

The Stanza

Some poems will have strophes that are more closely related to each other than they are to the surrounding strophes. We call a group of closely related strophes a stanza. Not all psalms will have stanzas. Psalm 111 does not. Stanzas tend to occur in longer psalms, like Psalm 139.

Psalm 139 is made up of two stanzas, verses 1–18 and verses 19–24. The first stanza is a reflection on the nature of God and is divided into three strophes. The first (vv. 1–6) reflects on God's knowledge, the second (vv. 7–12) on his presence, and the third (vv. 13–18) on his care. The second stanza is a response to this reflection and comprises two strophes. The first (vv. 19–22) is a resolution to be like God, and the second (vv. 23–24) is a request for an ever-deepening intimacy with God. As with strophes, so with stanzas: segmenting a poem into stanzas helps us to better understand the flow of the poet's thought and thereby helps us to better understand the poem.

Analyzing a poem in its constituent parts (cola, lines, strophes, stanzas) is basic to enjoying and understanding Hebrew poetry. We can now build on this foundation by taking a closer look at how Hebrew poets expressed their thoughts in parallel lines.

THOUGHTS IN PARALLELISM

Hebrew poets expressed their thoughts in poetic lines made from a number of cola. There is a certain flow of thought from one colon to the next, a particular relationship between the cola. We call this relationship parallelism.

What Is Parallelism?

Correspondence. Adele Berlin has said that the essence of parallelism is "correspondence."[2] Tremper Longman explains, "Parallelism refers to the correspondence which occurs between the phrases of a poetic line."[3] Longman uses the word *phrase* for what we are calling a colon, so parallelism is a relationship of correspondence between the cola of a poetic line.

The correspondence between the cola may be on the level of grammar, but such grammatical parallelism can be fully enjoyed and understood only while reading the poetry in Hebrew, since English grammar and Hebrew grammar are quite different.[4] The correspondence one can see while reading the poetry in translation is on the level of meaning.

Correspondence in Meaning. For our purpose, parallelism is the correspondence in meaning that exists between the cola of a poetic line. Let's look at Psalm 117:1 as an example.

> Praise the LORD, all you nations.
>   Extol him, all you peoples.

Note that "praise the LORD" corresponds to "extol him," and "all you nations" corresponds to "all you peoples." Another example is found in Psalm 118:28.

> You are my God, and I will give you thanks;
>   You are my God, and I will exalt you.

"You are my God" obviously corresponds to "you are my God" (although two different words are used for "God" in Hebrew). "I will give you thanks" corresponds to "I will exalt you." This verse illustrates that correspondence means the two cola are similar in meaning but not necessarily identical. And this leads us to probe more deeply into the way cola relate on the level of meaning.

How Does Parallelism Work?

An Older Understanding. An older understanding of Hebrew parallelism says that parallelism is the poetic technique of saying the same thing twice in different words. The examples we have looked at might lead you to believe that this understanding of how parallelism works is adequate. According to this older view, which you may have encountered in books or sermons, some parallel lines are synonymous (saying the same thing twice in different words) while other lines are antithetical (saying the same thing twice with opposite words like "remember . . . don't forget"). But then many lines were said to be synthetic, which meant that the second colon did not say the same thing again in either different or opposite words but added a new idea to the first colon. This category—synthetic—indicates that the older understanding does not do justice to the nature of the correspondence between the cola of a poetic line. In recent years a new understanding has been formulated.

A New Understanding. A new understanding of parallelism reflects more accurately, I think, how parallel lines work. I would put it this way: Parallelism is the art of saying something similar twice with a difference added in the second colon. The difference comes in a variety of shapes and sizes.

Let's look at several examples, beginning with Psalm 96:1.

> Sing to the LORD a new song;
>   sing to the LORD, all the earth.

The repetition of "sing to the LORD" establishes a fundamental correspondence between these two cola. In the context of this correspondence note the difference: The first colon tells us what is to be sung, and the second colon adds the idea of who is to do the singing. Compare this with Psalm 96:2.

> Sing to the LORD, praise his name;
>   proclaim his salvation day after day.

Here the second colon amplifies the idea of praising the name of God: We praise the name of God by proclaiming his salvation, and we praise the name of God day after day. Psalm 96:3 is similar.

> Declare his glory among the nations,
>   his marvelous deeds among all peoples.

"Among the nations" corresponds to "among all peoples." But what does "declare his glory" mean? How do we do that? The second colon supplies the needed information: We declare God's glory by declaring his marvelous deeds. His marvelous deeds are one aspect of his glory.

Let's look at two other poetic lines that are similar to each other. The first is Psalm 128:1.

> Blessed are all who fear the LORD,
>   who walk in his ways.

What does "fear the LORD" mean? The second colon provides us with at least one dimension of fearing the Lord: fearing the Lord is walking in his ways. The second colon adds information and thus helps us understand what the fear of the Lord is.

Then there is Psalm 112:1.

> Blessed is the man who fears the LORD,
> who finds great delight in his commands.

In this text, fearing the Lord is explained in terms of delighting in the Lord's commands. In our thinking "fear" and "delight" may seem to be mutually exclusive ideas, but that is not so in biblical thinking. By understanding how parallelism works, we come to understand that one key aspect of fearing the Lord is delighting in his commandments. By combining the teaching of Psalm 128:1 and Psalm 112:1 we learn that fearing the Lord is delighting in learning the Lord's commands and delighting in putting those commandments into practice in our daily living.

Let's look at one more example, Psalm 116:1.

> I love the LORD, for he heard my voice;
> he heard my cry for mercy.

Here the psalmist professes his love for the Lord because the Lord heard his voice. "Voice" is, however, a general term. The Hebrew word translated "voice" is used, for example, in expressions like "voice of thanksgiving" and "voice of joy" (see Pss. 26:7; 42:4; 47:1 NASB). What kind of voice did God hear in Psalm 116? The second colon says the voice was "a cry for mercy." God not only hears our voice when it speaks words of joyful thanksgiving; he also hears our voice when it is full of pain. And for this reason we love him.

When we read the poetic lines of a psalm slowly and by reflecting on how the second colon adds to the sense of the first, our understanding of the text deepens and our delight in the text blossoms. Understanding what parallelism is and how it works enriches our experience of hearing God speak to us through the Psalms.

PICTURES IN WORDS

"Poetry is the language of images," according to Leland Ryken.[5] And simply put, an image is a picture made out of words.[6] The high frequency of pictures painted with words is one factor that has made the message of the Psalms so accessible to God's people throughout the ages. I dare say that over the centuries the Book of Psalms has been read by God's people more than any other book in the Old Testament. And the primary reason for this is the use of imagery. To better understand and enjoy the images in the Psalms, we will consider three aspects of images.

Images Are Concrete

Images Are Pictures of Concrete Actions or Things. "The poets of the Bible constantly put us into a world of water and sheep and lions and rocks and arrows and grass."[7] Perhaps while you have read Exodus or Leviticus or Kings or Nahum, you have wondered what the content of these books has to do with your daily living. But when you read the Psalms, you almost immediately and intuitively see a relationship to your life. One of the reasons for this is the high frequency of imagery.

One of the first tasks in experiencing an image is to experience the concreteness of the image as fully as possible on a literal level. Before asking about the meaning of an image, it's helpful to sit with it and think about the literal picture.

The image in Psalm 11:1 provides a nice opportunity to practice experiencing the image on a literal level.

> In the LORD I take refuge.
> How then can you say to me:
> "Flee like a bird to your mountain."

Do not rush past these words, but stop at them. What picture comes to mind when you read, "Flee like a bird to your mountain"? The picture that comes to my mind is at the beach. My daughter and I were walking along the beach, and we saw sandpipers feeding at the water's edge. As Annie ran up to the birds, they immediately fled from her and landed at a safe distance. Getting a concrete picture in your mind's eye from your experience facilitates your understanding of the image and the meaning of the text.

What picture is evoked in your mind when you read Psalm 37:6?

> He will make your righteousness shine like the dawn,
> the justice of your cause like the noonday sun.

This past year I usually drove my oldest son to school at dawn. We drove west to his school; then I drove east to my office. Many mornings I drove with the brightly shining sun of a new dawn on the horizon. Morning skies in central Florida, where I live, can be spectacular. When you are in the right, even if all others think you are in the wrong, God will eventually make your righteousness shine like a spectacular dawn sky. Picture it in your mind.

David once said of God, "Your righteousness is like the mighty mountains" (Ps. 36:6). The picture that comes to my mind is that of the Canadian Rockies just west of Calgary, Alberta. Another picture that comes to mind is that of the Rock of Gibraltar. Or I can bring to mind standing at the base of El Capitan in Yosemite National Park. All are pictures of grandeur and strength, which give me insight into the Lord as a righteous God.

The first task when encountering an image is to experience that image as fully as possible on a literal level.

Images Can Have Different Meanings in Different Texts. A second principle to keep in mind is that the picture an image evokes in one text may be different from the picture evoked by the same image in a different text. We can use the image of snow as an illustration of this principle. In Psalm 51:7 we read,

> Cleanse me with hyssop, and I will be clean;
> wash me, and I will be whiter than snow.

This use of snow is meant to bring to your mind's eyes the whiteness of snow as a picture of purity. Snow is used in a different way in Psalm 68:14.

> When the Almighty scattered the kings in the land,
> it was like snow fallen on Zalmon.

Here the scattered nature of falling snow, not its color, is being evoked. This principle will help you not to misinterpret an image in one text based on its use in another. In each of these cases, the context guides you in determining what picture the image evokes. This becomes clearer as we consider how images work.

Images Have Three Parts. To better understand how an image works, let's look at the three components of an image: the topic, the vehicle, and the tenor.[8] We can use Psalm 10:9 to illustrate the three parts.

He lies in wait like a lion.

The *topic* is the subject about which the text is speaking. "He" is the topic of the image. The *vehicle* is the figurative part of the image, the part that transports the tenor. "Lion" is the vehicle. The *tenor* is the point of similarity between the topic and the tenor. The tenor is "lies in wait." Psalm 10:9 is rather straightforward, since all three parts are present. In some images, however, the tenor is not specified. The task of the interpreter is to determine which of a number of possible tenors is the point of similarity being evoked. To make this determination requires reflection.

Images Invite Reflection. Images are concrete, and we often connect with them immediately and intuitively. But images invite us to reflect on the point of similarity between the topic and the vehicle. This is always the case, especially when the tenor is left unstated. "The LORD is my shepherd," I am told in Psalm 23:1. But in what way or ways is the Lord my shepherd? Shepherds have many characteristics, and any one of these characteristics could hypothetically be the tenor. Reflection on this image in the context of the following lines leads to the conclusion that the Lord provides for me, guides me, and protects me, as a shepherd does for the sheep. Your task in reading a psalm is to figure out which of all possible tenors is the tenor that is being evoked in the poem. This takes practice.

Reflection Takes Practice. Let's practice on Psalm 5:9b.

Their throat is an open grave;
with their tongue they speak deceit.

The topic is "their throat," that is, the throats of David's adversaries. The vehicle is "an open grave." What is the tenor? When you think of an open grave, you might think of the danger of accidentally falling in and getting hurt. But graves in the ancient world were not dug in the ground, as ours are; they were hewn out of the side of a hill.[9] Since falling into a grave was not possible, the image is not that of danger or getting hurt. What if there were a body in a grave, a body that had been there for four days, as was the case with Lazarus (see John 11:17)? What would the grave be like if it were open? It would smell terrible (see John 11:39). "Stench" is the tenor in this image. "Their throat is foul like the stench of an open grave" is a fair translation. We will return shortly to this image to further probe its meaning. For now, let's be content to have discovered the tenor.

A second practice text is Psalm 127:4.

Like arrows in the hands of a warrior
are sons born in one's youth.

The topic is "sons," and the vehicle is "arrows." What is the tenor? Well, what are some characteristics of arrows? They are straight, skinny, and sharp. This last point is related to their use as a weapon of defense. The following line (v. 5) provides a clue for discovering the tenor.

Blessed is the man
whose quiver is full of them.

They will not be put to shame
when they contend with their enemies in the gate.

The picture is one of an older man in the city gate, which was the equivalent of a modern courthouse,[10] who is being falsely accused and who needs to be defended. And this father has ample defense, because his sons are there, at his side like a quiver full of arrows, to defend his cause. Sons are like arrows: a mighty source of defense.

A third practice text is Psalm 131:2.

But I have stilled and quieted my soul;
like a weaned child with its mother,
like a weaned child is my soul within me.

The topic is "my soul," and the vehicle is "a weaned child." Here the tenor is specified: "stilled and quieted." Reflecting imaginatively on an image like this one not only deepens our appreciation for the image but also facilitates our experience of the stillness and quietness the image envisions.

First, picture in your mind's eye a nursing baby, a hungry nursing baby, a hungry nursing baby strapped in the car seat of a car going 65 miles an hour down the freeway. Is this a picture of tranquility? Imagine the mother pulling off into a rest area and taking the baby from the car seat and holding the baby on her lap. Can you picture this baby—agitated and grasping at the breast to have her need for food satisfied? Not a picture of stillness and quietness, is it?

Now picture this same child at the age of five, weaned and no longer accustomed to going to the breast. Imagine this child, having just returned to the van after a long day at the amusement park, settled at her mother's side, content and quiet, tranquil and calm. That is a picture of the tranquility the Bible offers you in our fast-paced and hectic world.

For further practice you may wish to reflect on the images in Psalms 18:33, 32:9, 58:2, 66:10, 72:6, and 89:36–37 or other images that have captured your imagination. As you do so, reflect on how these images can be translated into your life, remembering that your reflection can be flexible.

Reflection Can Be Flexible. Since images are figurative and there is a general nature to them, there is flexibility in how you can apply them in your life. Take, for example, Paul's well-known "thorn in the flesh" (2 Cor. 12:7). The list of suggestions as to what this thorn refers to is as long as my arm. The fact is, we do not know what Paul's thorn was. In this case there is a benefit to not knowing. If we knew that this thorn was an eye ailment, as some interpreters have suggested based on Galatians 4:15, and you do not have an eye ailment, you would at a minimum find it more difficult to apply this text to your life. Not knowing what the thorn is facilitates the ease of application and expands the possibilities.

An example of this from the Book of Psalms is Psalm 23:2a.

> He makes me lie down in green pastures.

This is a picture of provision, the shepherd providing grass as food for the sheep. The immediate application is to trust the Lord to provide you with the food you need day by day, and there have been scores of believers throughout the ages who were not sure where their next meal was coming from. This image, however, can equally be applied to all sorts of situations. Whatever you need, the Lord will provide, as a shepherd provides for the sheep: spiritual maturity, finances, restored health in body or mind, relationships. The nature of imagery allows you to apply an image in a multiplicity of directions. Your reflection can be flexible.

Images Come in a Variety of Types

Two familiar kinds of images are similes and metaphors. Both are comparisons. A simile compares with the use of "like" or "as." We have already seen examples of a simile:

> Like arrows in the hands of a warrior
>   are sons born in one's youth. (Ps. 127:4)

A metaphor compares without the use of "like" or "as." Psalm 23:1 is an example:

> The LORD is my shepherd.

There are other kinds of images that are perhaps less familiar. Let's look at several of them.

Metonymy. Metonymy is the exchange of one noun for another with which it is commonly associated. A common example in English is the use of "the White House" to refer to the president of the United States. Let's return to our previous discussion of Psalm 5:9b.

> Their throat is an open grave;
>   with their tongue they speak deceit.

We have seen that "open grave" evokes the putrid stench of a rotting corpse. Our interest here is in the use of "throat." What is referred to by the word *throat*? The following colon provides the answer. The B colon indicates that the topic is the speech of David's adversaries. Since speech comes from the throat and is thus associated with the throat, "throat" can be used as a metonym for speech. The speech of the adversaries is full of deception and is thereby as foul as the stench of an open grave. The New Living Translation renders the verse,

> Their talk is foul, like the stench from an open grave.
> Their speech is filled with flattery.

The Hebrew word for "talk" literally means "throat" but is a metonym for "speech," and so the New Living Translation is justified in translating it with "talk." Note also that the New Living Translation speaks of the image of "open grave" in terms of "stench."

Another common example of metonymy is the use of "hand" for "power." Compare the New International Version and the New Living Translation at Psalm 17:7.

> Show the wonder of your great love,
> you who save by *your right hand*
> those who take refuge in you from their foes. (NIV)

> Show me your unfailing love in wonderful ways.
> You save with *your strength*
> those who seek refuge from their enemies. (NLT)

Since the hand is an obvious way one exerts power, "hand" can be used as a metonym for power.

Synecdoche. Synecdoche expresses the whole of something by referring to only a part of that whole, as in Psalm 44:6.

I do not trust in my bow,
  my sword does not bring me victory.

We would misunderstand the poet if we thought he did not trust in his bow or sword but did trust in his shield and chariot. Here "bow" and "sword" are synecdoches for military weaponry. This text can also be used to remind us of the flexible nature of imagery. If you do not use weapons, as the psalmist did, you might conclude that this text does not apply to you. "Bow" and "sword," more broadly speaking, however, represent human resources. So you can readily grasp this image as your profession of ultimate reliance on God rather than on your resources, whether those resources are athletic skills or interpersonal skills, intellectual ability or financial power, or any other resource. While you use these resources, you ultimately trust in the Lord, not the resources (see Ps. 127).

Hyperbole. Hyperbole is saying more than is literally intended. Some readers of the Bible may not be comfortable at first with the idea that the Bible uses hyperbole. This is because many of us were taught as children not to exaggerate because "exaggerating is lying." If all exaggerating is lying and hyperbole is exaggerating, then hyperbole is lying. However, hyperbole is not lying. Hyperbole is exaggeration for rhetorical impact. And in ordinary English conversation we use hyperbole *all the time*, as in an expression like "It took me *forever* to get home from the store today!"

One example of hyperbole is found in Psalm 107:26.

They mounted up to the heavens and went down to the
depths;
in their peril their courage melted away.

This text portrays sailors on the sea being tossed about in a horrific storm. The waves in this storm are so huge that they ascend all the way up into the heavens! More is being said here than is literally intended.

The word *all* is often used hyperbolically, as is the case in Psalm 118:10.

All the nations surrounded me,
but in the name of the LORD I cut them off.

The psalmist does not intend us to think that all the nations of the earth surrounded him or even that all the nations of the ancient Near East surrounded him. The poet uses the word *all* hyperbolically to refer with rhetorical power to the severity of the danger he was in while doing battle with a certain nation or possibly several nations.

Breviloquence. Breviloquence is related to the words *brief* and *eloquent* and is the omission of words for the sake of brevity. Breviloquence is "briefly eloquent." Consider Psalm 65:12–13.

The grasslands of the desert overflow,
the hills are clothed with gladness.
The meadows are covered with flocks
and the valleys are mantled with grain;
they shout for joy and sing.

As the first two cola of verse 13 make clear, this text envisions a successful year for the ancient farmer. The valleys are covered with grain, and the grasslands are filled with flocks. Verse 12 says that the "hills are clothed with gladness." Hills are not literally clothed with gladness. In fact, they are not literally clothed with anything. "Clothed" is a figure for "full of." The hills are literally filled with vegetation likes grasses and grains. Why then the reference to gladness? To say that "the hills are full of gladness" is to say with brief eloquence that "the hills are full of the grains and grasses that fill the farmer with gladness."

It is fascinating to realize that at all of the high points in creation and the history of redemption, there has been poetry. At the time of God's creating the heavens and the earth, the stars sang (Job 38:7). The exodus was memorialized in poetry (see Exod. 15). The poetry of Psalm 136 was recited at the dedication of the temple (see 2 Chron. 5:11–14). The day of salvation is a day commemorated with poetic song (see Isa. 12). The entrance of Christ into this world was celebrated with poetry (see Luke 1:46–55, 68–79; 2:14). And the end of history as we know it will include a panoply of poetry (see Rev. 4:8, 11; 5:9–10, 12, 13; 7:12; 11:15–18; 12:10–12; 13:10; 15:3–4; 16:5–7; 18:2–9, 16, 19–20, 21–24; 19:1–8). Poetry must be dear to the heart of God. May you grow in your understanding and enjoyment of the poetry of the Bible, so that you will grow in your understanding and enjoyment of the divine Poet, now and forever.

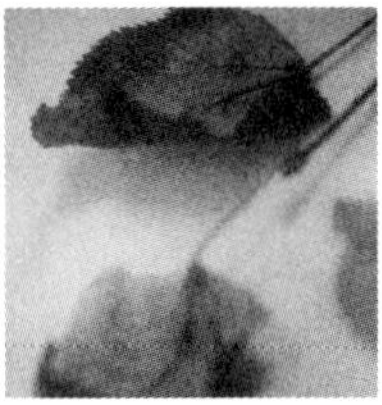

3

The Abundant Life

The Psalms as Instruction (Part 1)

Blessed is the man
who does not walk in the counsel of the wicked
or stand in the way of sinners
or sit in the seat of mockers.
But his delight is in the law of the LORD,
and on his law he meditates day and night.
He is like a tree planted by streams of water,
which yields its fruit in season
and whose leaf does not wither.
Whatever he does prospers.

Not so the wicked!
They are like chaff
that the wind blows away.
Therefore the wicked will not stand in the judgment,
nor sinners in the assembly of the righteous.

For the LORD *watches over the way of the righteous,*
but the way of the wicked will perish. (Ps. 1)

Why did God give us the Book of Psalms? This question has been answered in a variety of ways. For example, some interpreters understand the Book of Psalms to be an ancient hymnal, originally assembled for use in public worship. Others have taken the book to be devotional, originally used in private by individuals. The Book of Psalms has been used profitably in both ways throughout the history of the church. It is clearly the case that at least some if not many of the individual psalms were originally composed for use in worship. First Chronicles 16:7–36 strings together parts of Psalms 105, 96, and 106 and shows how they were used in public worship. But what was true for individual psalms may not have been the case with the book as a whole.

How might we discover the purpose of the Book of Psalms? We can often discover the purpose of a modern book by reading the introduction. If we had an ancient introduction to the Book of Psalms, that would be most helpful. I believe we have just such an introduction.

Psalms 1 and 2 stand at the beginning of the book and function as an introduction to it. There are several indicators of this. First, notice how through a number of key repetitions Psalms 1 and 2 have been bound together to form a tight unit. For example, the first word in the first line of Psalm 1 is the word *blessed*, and the first word in the last line of Psalm 2 is also the word *blessed*. Repeating the same word at the beginning and the end of a literary unity is a common technique in Hebrew poetry that is called an inclusion. This repetition serves to include all the material between in a single unit. Psalms 1 and 2 are bounded by an inclusion.

Note also the similar endings of Psalms 1 and 2. The last verse of Psalm 1 uses the words *way* and *perish* in the reference to those who do not live in harmony with God's way:

> But the way of the wicked will perish.

So too the last verse of Psalm 2 uses those same two words in reference to any who would refuse to submit to the Lord's authority:

> Kiss the son, lest you perish[1] in your way.

An interesting play on words also serves to tie the two psalms together. In Psalm 1:2, some people meditate. In Psalm 2:1, others plot. Guess what the Hebrew word for "plot" is? It is the same word that is translated "meditate" in Psalm 1:2! In Psalm 1, people meditate on God's Word in order to submit to it and live by it. In Psalm 2, people meditate on how to rebel against God's Word and live according to their own authority. The repetition of "blessed," "way/perish," and "meditate" serves to bind Psalms 1 and 2 together as a literary unity.

Not only are they bound together, but also they are separated from the psalms that follow. As the heading in most English translations indicates, Psalms 1–41 are book 1, the first of the five books of the Psalms. One thing that is interesting about book 1 is that Psalms 3–41 have "Of David" in the title. There are two apparent exceptions. There is no title to Psalm 10, but I think it can be demonstrated that Psalms 9 and 10 were originally one psalm that was accidentally divided in the history of transmission. There is also no title for Psalm 33, but if you read the last verses of Psalm 32,

> Rejoice in the LORD and be glad, you righteous;
> sing, all you who are upright in heart!

and the first verses of Psalm 33,

> Sing joyfully to the LORD, you righteous;
> it is fitting for the upright to praise him.

you can see how these two psalms have been linked by the repetition of key words like "LORD," "you righteous," "sing," and "upright," thus explaining why there is no title for Psalm 33. So, for practical purposes, we can say that Psalms 3–41 are all "of David."

If you look in your Bibles, what do Psalms 1 and 2 not have at the beginning? Neither has "Of David" as a title. Psalms like these first two have been called orphan psalms, because they have no title. Whereas key repetitions serve to bind Psalms 1 and 2 together, the lack of titles serves to set these two psalms apart from the following psalms of David. Psalms 1 and 2 have been purposely placed at the beginning of the Book of Psalms to serve as an ancient introduction to the book.

In chapter 5 we will look at the role Psalm 2 plays in introducing the Book of Psalms. Here our focus is on Psalm 1, as it teaches us that the Book of Psalms is fundamentally a manual for abundant living, experienced through godly living.

THE PSALMS: A MANUAL FOR ABUNDANT LIVING

Why do I say that Psalm 1 is a manual for abundant living? What in the text of the psalm leads to this conclusion? Two key factors result in understanding the Book of Psalms as a manual for abundant living. The first is the picture of blessedness that the poet paints, and the second is the promise of success found at the heart of the poem. Let's begin by looking at the picture of blessedness.

A Picture of Blessedness

The first word of Psalm 1, "blessed," is the key word of the psalm. The Hebrew word translated "blessed" is the word *ashrey*. This is different from the Hebrew word *barak*, which is used for God "blessing" people (see Ps. 5:12) and for people "blessing" God (see Ps. 103:1 in the NASB).[2] "Blessed," as it is used in Psalm 1, is not a word we use in modern English. So what does it mean in the ancient world of the psalmist? Psalm 1 gives us two keen insights.

Blessedness Is the Opposite of Perishing

First, blessedness is the opposite of perishing. And how do we know this? Notice that the first word of the psalm is "blessed" and that the last word of the psalm is "perish." Can you get any further apart in the psalm from the first word to the last? They are at the opposite ends of the psalm. The poet has placed these two words at opposite ends in the structure of the psalm to teach us poetically that "blessed" and "perish" are opposite in meaning.

Another detail in the Hebrew text underscores this contrast between "blessed" and "perish." The Hebrew word *ashrey* ("blessed") begins with the first letter of the Hebrew alphabet, aleph. And the Hebrew word *toveyd* ("perish") begins with the last letter of the Hebrew alphabet, tav. In the Hebrew alphabet you cannot get any further apart than aleph and tav. In the same way, you cannot get any further apart conceptually from the idea of blessedness and the idea of perishing.

The author of Psalm 1 is not the only poet to have used this technique. The composer of Psalm 112 has done the same. After the introductory "Praise the LORD," the first word of Psalm 112 is "blessed." And the last word of the psalm is the word *perish* (see NASB), which the New International Version translates "come to nothing." That Psalms 1 and 112 begin with "blessed" and end with "perish" is not accidental but is an intentional poetic device to give us insight into the meaning of "blessed." What is blessedness? Blessedness is the opposite of perishing.

Blessedness Is Like a Tree

Psalm 1 contains two contrasting similes that further our understanding of blessedness. Some people are "like chaff," and others are "like a tree." To perish is to be like chaff. Chaff has two characteristics that come to play in this image. Chaff vanishes. It is driven into oblivion by the wind. This is why the verse after this simile says,

> Therefore the wicked will not stand in the judgment,
> nor sinners in the assembly of the righteous.

Chaff is also good for nothing. In this psalm to perish is to vanish and to be good for nothing.[3] So the final colon of verse 6 can be translated "The path of the wicked will come to nothing."

As perishing is the opposite of blessedness, blessedness is the opposite of chaff. Blessedness is like a tree. In contrast to chaff, a tree has two characteristics that come to play in this image. A tree endures. When the winds blow,[4] a tree may bend but is not moved. And a tree is productive. It "yields its fruit in season."

These two similes add detail to the picture of blessedness. Blessedness is not living a life that vanishes into thin air, a life that ends up amounting to nothing. Blessedness is a life that is productive and makes a lasting difference, even an eternal difference.

Blessedness Is the Same as Happiness

Finding an English word to translate *ashrey* ("blessed") is not easy. As we have mentioned, "blessed" is not used in our ordinary conversations. Perhaps "truly happy" is the best English translation. I can think of two reasons for using the word *happy*. First, "happiness" is the English word that the major Hebrew dictionaries give when defining *ashrey*.[5] Scholars from different traditions, who have specialized in studying the meanings of Hebrew words, have concluded that "happy" is the best English word to capture the sense of *ashrey*.

Second, happiness is what people are looking for. I think if we are honest, happiness is high on the list of what we want in life. This is great! One reason that happiness is a high priority is because God created us to be happy.

To teach our children the basics of the Christian faith, my wife and I used a question-and-answer booklet. One question in the booklet is "In what estate [condition] did God create our first parents?" This answer follows: "God created our first parents happy and holy." The Garden of Eden was a perfectly happy place. The prophet Isaiah once promised that God would restore the ruined city of Jerusalem. To describe this restoration Isaiah said,

The LORD will surely comfort Zion
 and will look with compassion on all her ruins;
he will make her deserts *like Eden*,
 her wastelands *like the garden of the* LORD.
Joy and gladness will be found in her,
 thanksgiving and the sound of *singing*. (Isa. 51:3)

Eden was a place of uninterrupted "joy and gladness" and "thanksgiving" and "singing." We long to be happy because down in the recesses of our souls is a sense that we have been created for happiness.

In what sense are we using the word *happiness*? One meaning of *happiness* is "a state of well-being and contentment: joy." Happiness in this sense is how the Book of Psalms defines *ashrey*.

We have already noticed that, like Psalm 1, Psalm 112 begins with "blessed" and ends with "perish." Psalm 112 provides us with a brief though not exhaustive anatomy of blessedness. Verse 1 says,

Praise the LORD.

Blessed is the man who fears the LORD,
 who finds great delight in his commands.

The following verses flesh out the nature of this blessedness in terms of well-being in five significant areas of life.

Well-Being in Family

His children will be mighty in the land;
 the generation of the upright will be blessed. (v. 2)

The word translated "mighty" could be translated "warrior." These children are pictured as mighty warriors, victorious in all of life. The New Living Translation accordingly translates this colon, "Their children will be successful everywhere." This is the longing of the parental heart: that our children will succeed in all that they do. We do not send our children to school or sign them up for piano or swimming or basketball, hoping they will fail. We do not teach them the ways of the Lord, hoping they will fail to walk in those ways. We want our children to succeed in all areas of life, to be victorious, to experience blessedness.

Our children experience this blessedness, this well-being, because each "generation of the upright will be blessed." The word translated "blessed" in this colon is not *ashrey*. This word is related to the Jewish name Baruk, and the word means "to be empowered." It refers to being empowered by God to accomplish whatever he has created and redeemed us to do. This empowerment is for each generation that walks in God's ways.

Blessedness is well-being in the family.

Well-Being in Finances

Wealth and riches are in his house. (v. 3)

The second area in which well-being is experienced is in finances.

Just as Eden was a place of happiness, Eden was a place of wealth. The prophet Ezekiel says that "Eden, the garden of God" was a place of "every precious stone . . . ruby, topaz and emerald, chrysolite, onyx and jasper, sapphire, turquoise and beryl" (Ezek. 28:13). The river that flowed from Eden went to lands where there was exceptionally pure gold (Gen. 2:11–12). Wealth was part of God's original design for us, and heaven will be a place of such wealth that our streets will be paved with gold. The apostle John portrays heaven not as a garden but as a city. Yet, like the Garden of Eden, the heavenly city is a place of wealth.

> The wall was made of jasper, and the city of pure gold, as pure as glass. The foundations of the city walls were decorated with every kind of precious stone. The first foundation was jasper, the second sapphire, the third chalcedony, the fourth emerald, the fifth sardonyx, the sixth carnelian, the seventh chrysolite, the eighth beryl, the ninth topaz, the tenth chrysoprase, the eleventh jacinth, and the twelfth amethyst. The twelve gates were twelve pearls, each gate made of a single pearl. The great street of the city was of pure gold, like transparent glass. (Rev. 21:18–21)

Wealth in the time in between Eden and heaven is not a curse. In fact,

> The blessing of the LORD brings wealth,
> and he adds no trouble to it. (Prov. 10:22)

While the love of wealth and misplaced trust in wealth are to be avoided (see 1 Tim. 6:9–11, 17), wealth is to be enjoyed and shared (see 1 Tim. 6:17–18).

Blessedness is well-being in finances.

Well-Being in Spirit

> Wealth and riches are in his house,
> and his righteousness endures forever. (Ps. 112:3)

Immediately after mentioning wealth, the psalmist mentions righteousness. Spiritual well-being is a key component of blessedness. When I say "spiritual," I am not referring to one area of life that is isolated from other areas. Our spirituality penetrates and permeates our family life and our financial life and every other area of life. This spirituality, this righteousness is a matter of living in keeping with the principles that God has revealed to us. This is why Psalm 1 says that the blessed delight in and meditate on God's instruction on a regular basis (see chap. 4). This righteousness is not sinlessness, because the blessed are not those who never sin but those who process their sin in accordance with God's principles and thereby experience forgiveness.

> Blessed is he
> whose transgressions are forgiven,
> whose sins are covered. (Ps. 32:1)

The author of Psalm 112 mentions the kinds of qualities that characterize those who live in righteousness: they are upright, gracious, generous, and just in their dealings with others (vv. 4–5). The righteousness of which the psalmist speaks is not a flash in the pan, here today and gone tomorrow. True spirituality is an enduring righteousness, a righteousness that manifests itself day after day in all areas of life.

Blessedness is well-being in spirit.

Well-Being in Emotions

> He will have no fear of bad news;
> his heart is steadfast, trusting in the LORD.
> His heart is secure, he will have no fear;
> in the end he will look in triumph on his foes. (v. 7)

Well-being in our emotions doesn't mean that we are emotionless. Well-being in our emotions means that we are experiencing life as emotional creatures and expressing all of the emotions we experience in a way that is productive and healthy for us and for those around us. In fact, the Book of Psalms has been called "an anatomy of all the parts of the soul," because the Psalms bring to expression "all the griefs, sorrows, fears, doubts, hopes, cares, perplexities, in short, all the distracting emotions, with which the minds of men are wont to be agitated."[6] Take fear as an example. While "no fear" because of perfect "trust" may be our immediate response to a threatening person or situation, this is not always the case. David once said,

> When I am afraid,
> I will trust in you. (Ps. 56:3)

There are times when we fear, but by acknowledging that fear, as David did, and by trusting in God, as David did, we work through the fear to fearlessness, as David did:

> In God, whose word I praise,
> in God I trust; I will not be afraid. (Ps. 56:4)

The end of the process is in part what is in view in Psalm 112:7–8. Through the Book of Psalms, the Holy Spirit gives us the freedom to feel and the ways to feel so that our emotions are our servants and not our masters.

Blessedness is well-being in our emotions.

Well-Being in Body. Psalm 112 does not relate blessedness to well-being in the body, but Psalm 32 does. As we have already seen, Psalm 32 begins with the affirmation of the blessedness of sins forgiven. David goes on in verses 3–4 to describe what life was like when he was unwilling to deal with his sin according to God's principles.

> When I kept silent,
> my bones wasted away
> through my groaning all day long.
> For day and night
> your hand was heavy upon me;
> my strength was sapped
> as in the heat of summer.

Here we see a picture of the absence of well-being in body because of unconfessed sin. But when David confessed his sin, God forgave him (v. 5), and he experienced blessedness once again (vv. 1–2), and this blessedness in all likelihood included restored health. A parallel text to Psalm 32:1–5 is Job 5:17–18.

> Blessed is the man whom God corrects;
> so do not despise the discipline of the Almighty.
> For he wounds, but he also binds up;
> he injures, but his hands also heal.

David was corrected and disciplined by God by being wounded and injured. Did not the Lord then bind up those wounds and heal his injuries, as Job teaches? Or consider Psalm 103:3:

> [He] forgives all your sins
> and heals all your diseases.

Then there is the teaching of James 5:13–16.

> Is any one of you in trouble? He should pray. Is anyone happy? Let him sing songs of praise. Is any one of you sick? He should call the elders of the church to pray over him and anoint him with oil in the name of the Lord. And the prayer offered in faith will make the sick person well; the Lord will raise him up. If he has sinned, he will be forgiven. Therefore confess your sins to each other and pray for each other so that you may be healed. The prayer of a righteous man is powerful and effective.

Blessedness is well-being in the body.

Psalm 144:12–15 provides a beautiful though not comprehensive summary of blessedness as well-being:

> Then our sons in their youth
>   will be like well-nurtured plants,
> and our daughters will be like pillars,
>   carved to adorn a palace.
> Our barns will be filled
>   with every kind of provision.
> Our sheep will increase by thousands,
>   by tens of thousands in our fields;
>   our oxen will draw heavy loads.
> There will be no breaching of walls,
>   no going into captivity,
>   no cry of distress in our streets.
>
> Blessed are the people of whom this is true.
>   Blessed are the people whose God is the Lord.

What a beautiful picture of blessedness! It's the opposite of perishing. It's the same thing as happiness, in this deep, profound sense of well-being in every area of our lives. Blessedness is what God has created us for. Blessedness is what God has redeemed us for. Blessedness is what God is in the process of sanctifying us for, and blessedness is what he will glorify us for.

Blessedness Is a Key Theme in the Book of Psalms

The position of the word *ashrey* at the beginning and end of Psalms 1 and 2 signals the importance of blessedness in the theology of the Book of Psalms. The word *ashrey* occurs twenty-six times in the Psalms and is distributed throughout all five books. A sampling of occurrences will serve to illustrate the scope of usage and the importance of this theme.

Book 1: Psalm 40:4

Blessed is the man
who makes the LORD his trust,
who does not look to the proud,
to those who turn aside to false gods.

Book 2: Psalm 65:4

Blessed are those you choose
and bring near to live in your courts.
We are filled with the good things of your house,
of your holy temple.

Book 3: Psalm 84:4–5

Blessed are those who dwell in your house;
they are ever praising you.

Blessed are those whose strength is in you,
who have set their hearts on pilgrimage.

Book 4: Psalm 106:3

Blessed are they who maintain justice,
who constantly do what is right.

Book 5: Psalm 146:5

Blessed is he whose help is the God of Jacob,
whose hope is in the LORD his God.

The first word in the Book of Psalms, "blessed," is a key theme that runs through the book. The Book of Psalms was written as a manual to teach us how to experience the blessedness of which it speaks. Often we experience this blessedness in varying degrees and in the various aspects of our lives. While the lack of blessedness can often be traced, there may at times be a mysterious lack, a lack that transcends our current understanding, as was the case with Job. Job, however, seems not be to the rule but the exception. Let's live with the confident expectation not of the exception but of the rule, the picture held forth in the Book of Psalms from beginning to end:

O LORD Almighty,
happy [blessed] are those who trust you. (Ps. 84:12 NLT)

A Promise of Success

Closely related to the picture of blessedness painted in Psalm 1 is a promise we are given, a promise of success. Just as structural considerations are important for seeing the picture of blessedness, so too understanding the structure of the poem is essential to fully grasping the promise of success.

The Promise Is the Point of the Psalm

Psalm 1 is arranged in a special way. The name that has been given to this special arrangement is "chiasm." Chiasms are quite common in Hebrew poetry. A chiasm is a series (e.g., A, B, C) followed by the reverse of this series (e.g., C, B, A). If a chiastic poem has, for example, five strophes, the two outside strophes will be related to each other, then the next two strophes in will be related, and finally the central strophe will often contain the main point of the poem. A chiastic poem can be set out graphically as follows:

A
    B
        C
    B
A

Let's look at the chiastic structure of Psalm 1 to see what we can discover about the message of the poem. The outer strophes (vv. 1–2 and v. 5) contain two characterizations, the inner two strophes (v. 3a and v. 4b) contain two comparisons, and the central strophe (vv. 3b–4a) contains the main point.

Two Characterizations (vv. 1–2 and v. 5)

1 Blessed is the man
    who does not walk in the *counsel* of the **wicked**

or stand in the way of sinners
  or sit in the seat of mockers.
[2]But his delight is in the law of the LORD,
  and on his law he meditates day and night.

[5]Therefore the **wicked** will not stand in the judgment,
  nor sinners in the *assembly* of the righteous.

Notice the repetition of the words *wicked* and *sinners* in verses 1–2 and verse 5. The repetition of these key terms serves to tie these two strophes together. Next notice the words *counsel* (v. 1) and *assembly* (v. 5). There is a sound play between these two words, as the word for "counsel" is *a-tsat* and the word for "assembly" is *a-dat*. Only one sound distinguishes the two words. The poet used these two words that sound alike to further tie these strophes together.

Verses 1–2 provide us with a characterization of those who live in keeping with God's principles, while verse 5 characterizes those who do not.

Two Comparisons (v. 3a and v. 4b)

[3a]He is *like a tree* planted by streams of water,
  which yields its fruit in season
and whose leaf does not wither.

[4b]They are *like chaff*
  that the wind blows away.

These two strophes are related in that both contain similes signaled by the use of the word *like*. The similes are further connected in that both are images from the plant world, a tree and chaff. The connection is underscored in Hebrew, as the phrase "like a tree" sounds quite similar to the corresponding "like chaff." "Like a tree" is *ke-eyst*, and "like chaff" is *ka-mots*. Both begin with a *k*, which is followed by a single syllable that ends in *ts*. Can you hear the similarity? Those who live in keeping with God's principles are compared with a tree (*ke-eyst*), while those who do not are compared with chaff (*ka-mots*).

The Central Contrast (vv. 3b–4a)

3b Whatever he does prospers.

4a Not so the wicked!

Now we have arrived at the center of the poem and the main point. The main point is found in the contrast between those who prosper and those who do not. Those who live in keeping with God's principles are like trees and prosper; those who do not live according to God's principles are like chaff and do not prosper. Psalm 1 has been chiastically arranged to draw your attention to the main point at the center of the chiasm. The point of the poem contains a promise, and the promise is success.

The Point Is Success

In general, people want to succeed in life. We want our children to succeed in school, not to fail. We want them to win in athletics, not to lose. We get involved in starting a new church to have it grow, not to close it down after a year. We begin a business not to fail but to succeed. People want to succeed. Through the lens of Psalm 1, what can we learn about success?

Hebrew Tsalach *Means Succeed.* I think the Hebrew word translated "prospers" in verse 3b is better translated "succeeds."

One reason is because we tend to use the word *prosper* in the limited sense of financial success. But the Hebrew word *tsalach* is a broader term, just as "succeed" is a broader term than "prosper." The New International Version routinely uses "succeed" for Hebrew *tsalach* (see, e.g., Gen. 24:21; Judg. 18:15; 1 Chron. 22:13; Isa. 48:15; Jer. 32:5; Dan. 8:24).

Hebrew *tsalach* means to reach your goal, to accomplish what you set out to accomplish. A great example of this use is found in Isaiah 55:10–11.

> As the rain and the snow
> come down from heaven,
> and do not return to it
> without watering the earth
> and making it bud and flourish,
> so that it yields seed for the sower and bread for the eater,
> so is my word that goes out from my mouth:
> It will not return to me empty,
> but will accomplish what I desire
> and achieve [*tsalach*] the purpose for which I sent it.

God's Word comes down from heaven, and it does not return to heaven until it succeeds in doing exactly what God wants it to do. Hebrew *tsalach* means to achieve what we set out to achieve, to accomplish what we desire to accomplish. It means to succeed.

Second Chronicles 7:11 is another example of Hebrew *tsalach* meaning "succeed."

> When Solomon had finished the temple of the LORD and the royal palace, and had succeeded [*tsalach*] in car-

> rying out all he had in mind to do in the temple of the LORD and in his own palace . . .

To succeed is to accomplish everything you have in mind to do.

At the center of Psalm 1 is a remarkable promise: Those who live in keeping with God's principles succeed in whatever they set their minds to do!

Success Is an Aspect of Blessedness. The lead word in Psalm 1 is "blessed," and the central word is "success." These two terms help define each other. Well-being in all areas of life without success is hard if not impossible to imagine. Success without well-being is equally incomprehensible. If there is a difference between success and blessedness, success focuses on the process, and blessedness focuses on the result. Psalm 1 holds out the promise of success that results in well-being.

Success Is the Rule for the Righteous. Success is the rule for those who live in keeping with God's principles. This is the central affirmation of Psalm 1. Let's look at several other texts that support this idea. In 1 Chronicles 22:11 David prays for Solomon to succeed.

> Now, my son, the LORD be with you, and may you have success and build the house of the LORD your God, as he said you would.

Then two verses later David promises success to Solomon.

> Then you will have success if you are careful to observe the decrees and laws that the LORD gave Moses

> for Israel. Be strong and courageous. Do not be afraid or discouraged.

Notice that the promise of success is given in the context of Solomon living in keeping with God's principles. Later, in 1 Chronicles 29:23, we read how David's prayer was answered and his promise was fulfilled.

> So Solomon sat on the throne of the LORD as king in place of his father David. He prospered [*tsalach*] and all Israel obeyed him.

Similarly, with regard to King Uzziah, we read in 2 Chronicles 26:5,

> He sought God during the days of Zechariah, who instructed him in the fear of God. As long as he sought the LORD, God gave him success.

As we live in keeping with God's Word, we live with the confident expectation of succeeding in all that we do.

There Are Apparent Exceptions. We have seen that success is the rule for the righteous. Now we will consider several texts that indicate there are apparent exceptions. Psalm 37:7 says,

> Be still before the LORD and wait patiently for him;
> do not fret when men succeed in their ways,
> when they carry out their wicked schemes.

Here we are encouraged not to get upset when people succeed. Why would anyone get upset at the success of another? There are no doubt a number of answers to this question. This verse contains one of those answers in the third colon, which adds information to the second colon. The people who are succeeding in colon B are doing so through the "wicked schemes" of colon C, that is, through means that are not in keeping with God's principles. The reason this has the potential of upsetting some people is that Psalm 1 teaches that this is not supposed to happen. "Not so the wicked," says Psalm 1:4a; they don't succeed. The tension is heightened by the fact that the word translated "succeed" in Psalm 37:7 is the identical word translated "succeeds" in Psalm 1.

A second text is Jeremiah 12:1.

> You are always righteous, O LORD,
>   when I bring a case before you.
> Yet I would speak with you about your justice:
>   Why does the way of the wicked prosper?
>   Why do all the faithless live at ease?

In a bold prayer the prophet Jeremiah acknowledges his belief in the righteousness of God. The prophet knows that God always acts in keeping with his own principles, yet there is something going on in Jeremiah's world that is apparently not in keeping with divine principles. Jeremiah wants to know "Why does the way of the wicked prosper?" Again, the word translated "prosper" is the same word used for "succeeds" in Psalm 1, and in Psalm 1:6 the "way of the wicked" does not prosper but perishes. Colon C in Jeremiah 12:1 adds to the intensity, especially when we realize that the Hebrew word translated "faithless" could be translated "those who act treacherously." The way of treacherous people is succeeding—it is not supposed to be this way.

There may be times when we cannot figure out how God's promise of success and the circumstances of life fit together in a harmonious whole. But let's remember that any apparent exceptions only serve to underscore the rule. "The prosperity of the wicked" (add conversely the suffering of the righteous) is a problem only if this is not the way it is supposed to be in God's world. The exception proves the rule. God's promise of success stands.

Let's conclude with a prayer, not from the Book of Psalms but from the New Testament—a prayer that concisely summarizes the teaching of Psalm 1 to this point. May this prayer be the prayer of our hearts for ourselves and for others, as it was the prayer of the apostle John for his dear friend Gaius.

> Beloved, I pray that in all respects you may prosper and be in good health, just as your soul prospers. (3 John 2 NASB)

This is the abundant life that Jesus came to give us (John 10:10).

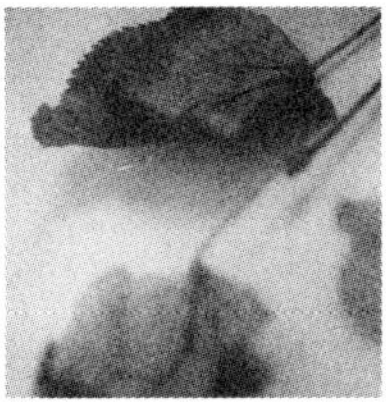

4

THE GODLY LIFE

The Psalms as Instruction (Part 2)

Blessed is the man
who does not walk in the counsel of the wicked
or stand in the way of sinners
or sit in the seat of mockers.
But his delight is in the law of the LORD,
and on his law he meditates day and night.
He is like a tree planted by streams of water,
which yields its fruit in season
and whose leaf does not wither.
Whatever he does prospers.

Not so the wicked!
They are like chaff
that the wind blows away.
Therefore the wicked will not stand in the judgment,
nor sinners in the assembly of the righteous.

For the LORD watches over the way of the righteous,
but the way of the wicked will perish. (Ps. 1)

I have already mentioned the question-and-answer booklet that my wife and I used to teach our children the basics of the Christian faith. When we asked, "In what estate [condition] did God create our first parents?" one of the children, not familiar with the word *estate*, answered questioningly, "Maryland?" Marylanders might like that answer, but the correct answer is "God created our first parents happy and holy." In the previous chapter we have learned that the Book of Psalms is a manual for teaching us how to be happy, that is, how to live the abundant life that God has created us and redeemed us to live. In this chapter our focus is on the second half of the answer, holy. Simply put, happiness and holiness go together. In God's economy the abundant life is experienced more and more as we live more and more in keeping with divine principles. The abundant life is at the same time the godly life.

Psalm 1 gets at this idea of the godly life in two related ways. This psalm invites us to delight in and meditate on divine principles for living found first and foremost in the Psalms and also by extension in the whole of the Bible.

A Call to Delight in the Lord's Instruction

Torah Means Instruction

Psalm 1:2 refers to "the law of the LORD," and the word translated "law" is the Hebrew word *torah*. It is interesting to me that while most modern translations typically use the English word *law* to translate the Hebrew word *torah*, the standard Hebrew dictionaries all list the word *teaching* or *instruction* as well as and even prior to the word *law*. Moreover, the Hebrew verb that is related to the noun *torah* means "to teach" or "to instruct." It seems that the word *torah* first meant "instruction" and then came to mean an "established instruction" or a "law." In other words, "law" is a specialized kind of instruction, and the more general word *instruction* is a better choice for Psalm 1:2.

Translators have used the word *teaching* in a number of places to translate *torah*. "Teaching" as a translation of *torah* is most common in the Book of Proverbs. For example, Proverbs 1:8 says,

> Listen, my son, to your father's instruction
> and do not forsake your mother's teaching [*torah*].

Similarly Proverbs 3:1 says,

> My son, do not forget my teaching [*torah*],
> but keep my commands in your heart.

Other examples are found in Proverbs 4:2; 6:20, 23; and 13:14 (see also Mal. 2:8). Closer to home for Psalm 1 is Psalm 78:1, where we read,

> O my people, hear my teaching [*torah*];
> listen to the words of my mouth.

Interestingly enough, Psalm 78 and Psalm 1 share characteristics in common with the wisdom literature of the Book of Proverbs. For example, Psalm 1 describes "two ways" people can follow in life, the way of the righteous and the way of the wicked. These two ways are found repeatedly in the wisdom teaching of Proverbs, as a quick comparison makes clear:

> But *the way of the wicked* is like deep darkness;
> they do not know what makes them stumble. (Prov. 4:19)

> I walk in *the way of righteousness*,
> along the paths of justice. (Prov. 8:20)

As in Proverbs, so in Psalm 1:2, "the *torah* of the LORD" refers to "the instruction of the LORD."

INSTRUCTION IS FOUND IN TWO KEY PLACES

If abundant living comes through delighting in "the instruction of the LORD," a natural question arises: Where can I find this instruction? While this question can be answered in a variety of ways, two dimensions of the answer are central for understanding Psalm 1 and the Book of Psalms.

Found in the Five Books of Moses

First, "the instruction/*torah* of the LORD" is found in the five books of Moses (Genesis, Exodus, Leviticus, Numbers, and Deuteronomy). In Christian tradition these five books are known as the Pentateuch, which means "five-part scroll." In Jewish tradition they are known simply as the Torah. When the first readers of the completed Book of Psalms read Psalm 1, they would have understood "the instruction/*torah* of the LORD" to refer to the Torah, the five books of Moses.

The individual psalms were written over a span of about a thousand years. Psalm 90 was written by Moses (1526–1406 B.C.), and Psalm 137 was written some time after the return from the Babylonian captivity in 539 B.C. The Book of Psalms grew over the years as new psalms were added. The collection would have been put in its final form sometime around the days of Ezra and Nehemiah, perhaps around 400 B.C. Let's look at one of the ways the people at that time used the word *torah*.

In Ezra 7:6 we read,

> This Ezra came up from Babylon. He was a teacher well versed in the instruction [*torah*] of Moses, which the LORD, the God of Israel, had given.

Here on the one hand the *torah* is called "the *torah* of Moses," and on the other hand it is called the *torah* "which the LORD, the God of Israel, had given." So "the *torah* of Moses" is "the *torah* of the LORD." Second Chronicles 34:14, written around the time of Ezra and Nehemiah, reverses the language:

> While they were bringing out the money that had been taken into the temple of the LORD, Hilkiah the priest found the Book of the Law [*torah*] of the LORD that had been given through Moses.

Here the *torah* is called "the *torah* of the LORD," and it is the *torah* given through Moses. So "the *torah* of the LORD" is "the *torah* of Moses."

In the days of Ezra and Nehemiah the first readers of the Book of Psalms would have naturally understood "the instruction/*torah* of the LORD" to refer to "the instruction/*torah* of

Moses." At a minimum "the instruction/*torah* of Moses" would have referred to the Book of Deuteronomy, but the following discussion will show that the reference is to the five books of Moses.[1]

It can be fairly said that the five books of Moses were given to teach God's people how to live an abundant life in the Promised Land. It is beyond the scope of this book to provide a full demonstration of this point, but we learned in the previous chapter that we were created to live in the Garden of Eden, a place of great abundance (Gen. 1–2). In addition it is clear that Israel was called to live in a land of abundance. This abundance is described for us in Deuteronomy 8:7–9:

> For the LORD your God is bringing you into a good land—a land with streams and pools of water, with springs flowing in the valleys and hills; a land with wheat and barley, vines and fig trees, pomegranates, olive oil and honey; a land where bread will not be scarce and you will lack nothing; a land where the rocks are iron and you can dig copper out of the hills.

Fifteen times in the Old Testament, the land is called a "good land," as it is in Deuteronomy 8:7. Nineteen times this abundance is referred to metaphorically as the "land flowing with milk and honey" (e.g., Exod. 3:8; Deut. 6:3; 11:9). Instructions for living the abundant life are found in the five books of Moses, but that is not the only place this instruction is found.

Found in the Five Books of the Psalms

The first people to read the Psalms when the book was newly completed would have understood a second referent when they read "the instruction/*torah* of the LORD." They would have understood that this instruction is found in the Book of Psalms.

In the ancient Hebrew tradition that goes back to the days when the Book of Psalms was put in its final form, the Psalms were divided into five books. Most modern translations indicate this fivefold division by inserting, for example, something like "Book 1 (Psalms 1–41)" just before Psalm 1. Similar headings will be found just before Psalms 42, 73, 90, and 107. Why at these psalms?

It is not the beginning but the ending of each book that contains the ancient marker that divides the Psalms. Books 1–4 are all brought to a close by a similar doxology.

Psalm 41:13

Praise be to the LORD, the God of Israel,
from everlasting to everlasting.
Amen and Amen.

Psalm 72:18–19

Praise be to the LORD God, the God of Israel,
who alone does marvelous deeds.
Praise be to his glorious name forever;
may the whole earth be filled with his glory.
Amen and Amen.

Psalm 89:52

Praise be to the LORD forever!
Amen and Amen.

Psalm 106:48

Praise be to the LORD, the God of Israel,
from everlasting to everlasting.
Let all the people say, "Amen!"

The word *amen* occurs in the Psalms only in these doxologies, so these unique verses clearly mark the ends of the first four books. Book 4 closes with the exclamation "praise the LORD!" This exclamation, as we have seen in chapter 1, marks the beginning and the ending of each of Psalms 146–150, which thus form a grand doxology to book 5 and to the entire Book of Psalms.

The question arises: Why a fivefold division? Why not four or six sections? The answer is that the fivefold Book of Psalms is intended to mirror the fivefold books of Moses. This does not mean that we should look for parallels between book 1 of the Psalms and Genesis. The point is, rather, that just as the five books of Moses are "the instruction/*torah* of the LORD," so are the five books of the Psalms.

Like the five books of Moses, the five books of the Psalms have at the center of their purpose the function of being a manual of instruction in general and instruction on how to live the abundant life in particular. It is appropriate to sing the psalms in the public worship of God, but we must not lose sight of God's intention for us to gain instruction on abundant living as a key component of his reason for giving us the Psalms. Paul understood this when he said in Colossians 3:16,

> Let the word of Christ dwell in you richly as you teach and admonish one another with all wisdom, and as you sing psalms, hymns and spiritual songs with gratitude in your hearts to God.

The Psalms are for teaching people how to live a godly and abundant life.

Instruction Is Our Delight

Instruction and delight do not always go together in people's minds, but they went together very well in the minds of the psalmists. Psalm 1:2 sets the stage when it says that our "delight is in the law [instruction] of the LORD." The blessedness of Psalm 1 is also, as we have seen, the theme of Psalm 112, and Psalm 112:1 leads us to delight in God's instruction,

> Blessed is the man who fears the LORD,
>   who finds great delight in his commandments.

This delighting in God's instruction runs like a golden thread through Psalm 119. Nine times in this psalm God's instruction is said to be our delight (vv. 16, 24, 35, 47, 70, 77, 92, 143, 174). And nine times God's instruction is said to be the object of our love (vv. 47, 48, 97, 113, 119, 127, 159, 163, 167). We delight in God's instruction because we love it (Ps. 119:47), and we love it because, among other reasons, we know that his instruction is the path to life and peace (Ps. 119:77, 165). Living in keeping with God's instructions is the way to abundant living.

The well-being and success of which Psalm 1 speaks comes to us through our delighting in God's instruction. Joshua 1:8 says, "Do not let this Book of the Law [Instruction/*torah*] depart from your mouth; meditate on it day and night. . . . Then you will be prosperous and successful." It's our delight because it leads to success and blessedness (see also 1 Chron. 22:13).

So the Psalms issue us a call to delight in God's instruction. His instruction is good, and it is for our benefit. It doesn't hinder us or restrict us. The Bible doesn't say that you'll know the truth and the truth will restrict you and keep you from reaching your full potential in life. Instead, "You will know the truth, and the truth will set you free" (John 8:32). Free to live. Free to live out your divine purpose. Free to experience the abundant life that Jesus came to give.

This delighting in God's instruction has an emotional side to it. To delight in God's instruction is to enjoy that instruction, as Psalm 119:111 says:

> Your statutes are my heritage forever;
> they are the joy of my heart.

In addition to this, delighting in God's instruction has a practical side to it. One practical outworking of delighting in God's instruction is the practice of meditating on that instruction, a practice that Psalm 1 mentions and to which we now turn.

A CALL TO MEDITATE ON THE LORD'S INSTRUCTION

Psalm 1:2 pairs up delighting in and meditating on God's instruction.

> But his delight is in the law of the LORD,
> and on his law he meditates day and night.

This same pair is found in Psalm 119:15–16, which says,

> I meditate on your precepts
> and consider your ways.

I delight in your decrees;
    I will not neglect your word.

Then there is Psalm 119:47–48:

. . . for I delight in your commands
    because I love them.
I lift up my hands to your commands, which I love,
    and I meditate on your decrees.[2]

Psalm 1 calls us to a delightful mediation on God's instruction. What does that meditation look like? Since Psalm 1 begins by outlining what people who want to experience the abundant life avoid before it details what they embrace, we will do the same.

AVOIDING THE WRONG ADVICE

Psalm 1 opens with an extended metaphor that paints a negative picture for a positive purpose. The negativity is expressed in two ways. The first and obvious way is the threefold repetition of "not." Most English translation use "not . . . or . . . or," so the threefold repetition found in the Hebrew text is somewhat obscured. The New American Standard Bible and the New King James Version use "not . . . nor . . . nor," and this highlights the negativity of the original text a bit better. The abundant life is experienced in part by what we do not, not, not do.

The second and more nuanced way the negativity is expressed is in the sequence of the three verbs *walk*, *stand*, and *sit*. Walking leads to standing, which leads to sitting. A downward spiral is placed before us. Activity slows to passivity. Life grinds to a halt.

These three verbs are used with the three key nouns *counsel*, *way*, and *seat*. Walking in the counsel is a metaphor for yielding to influences. Standing in the way speaks of following patterns of behavior. Seating in the seat stands for taking on an attitude. Negative influences lead to negative behaviors, which lead to negative attitudes.

Influences

Influence is the power of causing an effect in indirect or intangible ways. Influence is a subtle form of power because of its indirect and intangible nature. We are bombarded by potential influences all day long. Some will move us forward on the path of blessedness. Others will move us downward on the path of perishing. Subtle though the power of influence may be, we always choose what influences we will yield to and what influences we will say no to. Psalm 1 presumes we will be exposed to negative influences, to "the counsel of the wicked." Psalm 1 encourages us not to yield to that kind of influence.

It would be an oversimplification to equate the "counsel of the wicked" with the advice of non-Christians. In the Book of Psalms the "wicked" are frequently people who are members of the covenant community, as Psalm 50:16 makes clear:

> But to the wicked, God says:
>
> "What right have you to recite my laws
> or take my covenant on your lips?"

The wicked here are those who, though they live in the covenant community, do not live in keeping with God's instruction, as is plain from the following verse:

> "You hate my instruction
>   and cast my words behind you." (v. 17)

A second reason is that by God's common grace non-Christians can and do give advice that moves us forward on the path of blessedness. Avoiding negative influences is not as simple as avoiding non-Christians and following what Christians say. Avoiding negative influences is a matter of discerning the truth of divine principles no matter what the source.

The primary way we gain this discernment in Psalm 1 is by delighting in and meditating on God's instructions in the five books of Moses, in the five books of the Psalms, and even more broadly in the whole of the Scriptures. Equipped with knowledge of the Lord's instruction in the Bible, we are in a position to avoid wrong advice and to "cling to what is good" (Rom. 12:9).

Behaviors

Influence causes an effect. The effect in view in Psalm 1 is on our behavior. By not yielding to negative influences, we stay off of the "way of sinners."

The "way" refers to a pattern of behavior or a lifestyle rather than to a single act. The "way of sinners" refers to any pattern of behavior that is out of keeping with God's instruction. There are two ways, according to Psalm 1: the way that leads to blessedness and the way that leads to nothingness. Jeremiah 21:8 puts it this way:

> This is what the LORD says: See, I am setting before you the way of life and the way of death.

The "way of sinners" is the "way of death," which is the opposite of the "way of life." The "way of life" is the "way of the LORD." Speaking of Abraham in Genesis 18:19, God says,

> For I have chosen him, so that he will direct his children and his household after him to keep the way of the LORD by doing what is right and just, so that the LORD will bring about for Abraham what he has promised him.

The way of the Lord is doing what is right. And walking in the way of the Lord brings the promises of the Lord to realization in our lives. By not yielding to negative influences, we do not develop negative behaviors and life does not grind to a halt. The intent of Psalm 1 is to motivate us to yield to the influence of God's instruction in how we act throughout the day so that we experience the life that God intends for us.

Attitudes

Influences also affect attitudes. If someone chooses to yield to negative influences, negative patterns of behavior are sure to follow. These negative patterns of behavior over time produce negative attitudes, and the downward spiral is complete.

When I was young, to say that someone "had an attitude" required qualification. Good or bad? These days to "have an attitude" means to have a bad attitude. The bad attitude in view in Psalm 1 is that of the "mocker" or "scoffer." This person is referred to in the Book of Psalms only here. The "scoffer" is encountered much more often in the Book of Proverbs. To scoff is to be foolish (Prov. 19:29) and not wise (Prov. 13:1). It is to resent being corrected (Prov. 15:12) and to hate God's instruction (Prov. 1:22). To scoff is to have a fundamental and pervasive arrogance (Prov. 21:24) that refuses to live in keeping with God's instruction. The scoffer's attitude thus leads to a yielding to negative influences that further the downward spiral of patterns of behavior that produce death.

Psalm 1 envisions an abundant life of success in all that we do. The degree to which we experience this abundance is in large measure determined by choices that we make. What influences will we yield to? What patterns of behavior will we develop? What fundamental attitudes will we foster and live out of? Psalm 1 encourages us to turn from the influences, behaviors, and attitudes that are not in harmony with God and the blueprint for life he has given us in the Scriptures.

Avoiding the wrong advice is, however, only one perspective and a negative one at that. Psalm 1 also provides us another, positive perspective on the foundation of an abundant life: absorbing the right advice.

ABSORBING THE RIGHT ADVICE

Meditation is a practice that is growing in popularity in our culture, if not in the church. Books and tapes about meditation abound. Psalm 1 is not a manual on meditation, but it does provide a few key insights into the nature of mediation as practiced in ancient Israel. These insights prove helpful for people living in the twenty-first century.

Meditating with Your Mouth

The Old Testament has several Hebrew words that are translated "meditate." The primary word for "meditate," used in Psalm 1:2, is *hagah*. This Hebrew word typically refers to a vocal activity. With an animal as the subject, the verb can mean "coo" (Isa.

38:14) or "growl" (Isa. 31:4). When humans are the subject, the verb can refer to either articulate speech (Isa. 59:3) or a muttering that might resemble the cooing of a dove or the low growling of a lion. This latter sense provides our first insight into biblical meditation: we can meditate with our mouths.

To meditate is to read in an undertone or to mutter the words of the Bible while contemplating their significance for our lives. Perhaps you can picture a Hasidic Jew at the Western Wall in Jerusalem reading a Hebrew Bible, and maybe you can even hear in your mind's ear that person's low, rumbling recitation of the Word of God. Such a recitation of Scripture is part of meditation. This explains why the Lord said to Joshua, "Do not let this Book of the Law depart from your mouth; meditate on it day and night" (Josh. 1:8). Similarly Psalm 19:14 couples "the words of my mouth" and "the meditation of my heart." Meditation and vocalization belong together. You meditate on the Book by reciting the words of the Book with your mouth.

As a professor of Hebrew I encourage my students to learn their Hebrew vocabulary with as many senses as possible. With their hands they can write the words, with their eyes they can see them, and with their ears they can hear them when they recite them aloud with their mouths. The use of multiple senses helps them sink the words more deeply into the memory. So too, as we meditate aloud on the Word of God, that Word sinks more deeply into our memory and into our hearts.

Meditating with Your Heart

Meditation is more than reciting God's Word with our mouths. Meditation involves the heart. We have already encountered the connection between meditation and the heart in Psalm 19:14, which refers to the "meditation of my heart."

To Meditate Is to Think. The Hebrew word often translated "heart" is *leb* (pronounced like "save"). In addition to referring to the physical heart (1 Sam. 25:37), the word *leb* can also refer to the seat of human emotions (Exod. 4:14; 1 Sam. 2:1). Hebrew *leb* can also be used for the seat of human reasoning (Deut. 29:3; Neh. 5:7; Job 12:3; Prov. 23:23). While not excluding the emotions, the "meditation of my heart" in ancient Israel included thoughts. To meditate was to think.

Notice the parallel verbs in Psalm 77:12:

> I will meditate on all your works
> and consider all your mighty deeds.

Meditating on God's works is explained in terms of considering or thinking about his mighty deeds. This explains why the Hebrew word *hagah* is at times translated "think," as in Psalm 63:6:

> On my bed I remember you;
> I think of you through the watches of the night.

The New American Standard Bible, the New King James Version, and the New Revised Standard Version all use the word "meditate" here, where the New International Version uses "think." Just as the verb *remember* refers to mental activity, so does the corresponding verb *hagah* ("think" or "meditate").

To meditate on a text of Scripture is to think about that text. While meditating, our minds are active and engaged, considering, pondering, thinking about the meaning of God's Word for our day-to-day living.

To Meditate Is to Think Deeply. To meditate is more than thinking. To meditate is to think deeply. To meditate is to think reflectively about the Word of God. It is to take the Word of God and turn it over and over in your mind, probing the Word for its significance, asking how it applies to your life, pondering the kind of personal transformation the Word is to produce within you. One of your goals in meditating is an increased ability to live in keeping with the instructions you are meditating on. This is why the Lord said to Joshua (Josh. 1:8),

> Do not let this Book of the Law depart from your mouth; meditate on it day and night, so that you may be careful to do everything written in it.

To gain insight into the meaning of Scriptures for your life often takes deep thought; thus the psalmist (Ps. 119:99) can say,

> I have more insight than all my teachers,
> for I meditate on your statutes.

Sometimes you are engaged in this kind of deep thought for long stretches of time, as in Psalm 119:148:

> My eyes stay open through the watches of the night,
> that I may meditate on your promises.

And Psalm 63:6 says,

> On my bed I remember you;
> I think of you through the watches of the night.

Meditating throughout the night. Meditating day and night. To meditate is to think deeply.

To Meditate Is to Think Deeply in the Spirit. To meditate is more than even thinking deeply. To meditate is to think deeply in the Spirit. While meditation is a human activity, it has a decided divine dimension. We meditate in communion with the Holy Spirit.

Teachers are good but not necessary. What do I mean by that? When Jesus ascended to heaven after his resurrection from the dead, he appointed teachers in the church (Eph. 4:8–13). Teachers have a vital role to play in the church; otherwise Jesus would not have put them in place. Teachers are good.

But there's another perspective, as shown in 1 John 2:27:

> As for you, the anointing you received from him remains in you, and you do not need anyone to teach you. But as his anointing teaches you about all things and as that anointing is real, not counterfeit—just as it has been taught you, remain in him.

John is not giving this teaching at a conference for pastors. Rather, he is talking to all believers. All believers have an anointing so that they can be taught directly by the Holy Spirit without a human teacher. Do you believe this? Do you believe that there is a real anointing of the Holy Spirit for all believers, for you?

This anointing is at work while you meditate. Meditation is more than your deep reflections on the meaning of the Word of God for your life. In some mysterious way, the Holy Spirit works through the Word and in your thoughts to teach you how to live a godly life that is also an abundant life. Jesus said that if we drink the water he offers us, we will never be thirsty. That water will become in us a spring of water welling up to eternal life (John 4:14). This eternal life is the abundant life Jesus came to give (John 10:10), and the water of eternal and abundant life that wells up within us also flows from us to others (John 7:38). And this water is the Holy Spirit (John 7:39).

As we meditate we are thinking deeply about the words on the pages of Scripture, and we are listening intently to hear the voice of the Spirit. He is present within us to teach us everything we need to know to live in keeping with God's instructions and to experience all of the life that God has for us, in this life and in the life to come.

The abundant life is the godly life. The two go together, and the Book of Psalms is an instruction manual for both. It is a manual given to you by God to provide you with instruction for abundant and godly living. Psalm 1 paints a picture of happiness, and it promises you success. This happiness and success are rooted in living by divine principles.

Psalm 1 and the Book of Psalms would be misunderstood if you were to think that in order to be successful and truly happy the only thing you need to do is never submit to negative influences, never engage in negative behaviors, and never develop a bad attitude. Who has that kind of track record?

Jesus does! *Jesus never once submitted to the wrong influences.* When he was in the wilderness, he was given bad advice time and time again. But he always countered that advice with the instruction of God, instruction from the Book of Deuteronomy in particular (one of the five books of Moses). Jesus had apparently meditated on God's instruction. He had thought deeply in the Spirit and had consistently followed God's instruction. *Jesus never once engaged in the wrong behaviors*. He was tempted in every way, just as you and I are, but he never violated God's principles, not even once (Heb. 4:15). *Jesus never developed a scornful attitude toward his Father's will*. He humbly submitted to his Father's will, even to the point of dying on the cross (Luke 22:42).

Jesus lived the perfectly godly life that is required for the abundant life of which Psalm 1 speaks. He lived the godly life in our place and earned the abundant life for us. He died to remove our sins and their consequences from us and was raised to pour out his Spirit into us that we might live the godly life more and more and experience the abundant life more and more. The abundant and godly lives that we now live we live by faith in Jesus, who loved us and gave himself for us (Gal. 2:20).

Psalm 1 is a call for you to experience all of the blessedness and all of the success that God has for you in Christ—in the power of his Spirit and based on his person and work.

Jesus said (John 10:10 NASB),

> The thief comes only to steal and kill and destroy; I came that they may have life, and have it abundantly.

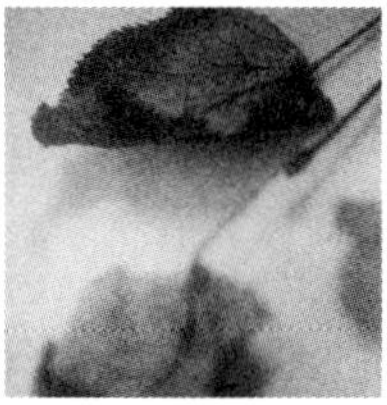

5

The Lord Reigns

The Psalms of the Kingdom

Why do the nations conspire
and the peoples plot in vain?
The kings of the earth take their stand
and the rulers gather together
against the LORD
and against his Anointed One.
"Let us break their chains," they say,
"and throw off their fetters."

The One enthroned in heaven laughs;
the Lord scoffs at them.
Then he rebukes them in his anger
and terrifies them in his wrath, saying,
"I have installed my King
on Zion, my holy hill."

I will proclaim the decree of the LORD*:*

He said to me, "You are my Son;
today I have become your Father.
Ask of me,
and I will make the nations your inheritance,
the ends of the earth your possession.
You will rule them with an iron scepter;
you will dash them to pieces like pottery."

Therefore, you kings, be wise;
be warned, you rulers of the earth.
Serve the LORD with fear
and rejoice with trembling.
Kiss the Son, lest he be angry
and you be destroyed in your way,
for his wrath can flare up in a moment.
Blessed are all who take refuge in him. (Ps. 2)

When we look around at the world in which we live, it is all too easy to see war and crime and disease and death. A natural question enters our minds: Is there a good God in control of this world? At times there seems to be an abundance of evidence for answering no.

In this regard things are no different now than they were when the Book of Psalms reached its final form in the days after the Babylonian captivity. Although the Scriptures had taught the people of God that the Lord was reigning over them and over the world in which they lived, there was much evidence to the contrary. If the Lord was reigning, why were his people not a dominant world power, as they had been in the days of David and Solomon? Why were they a small, poor province in the large and prosperous Persian Empire? Where was the abundant life promised in Psalm 1? The Book of Psalms was composed to address these kinds of theological questions for the original audience and for us.

The message of the Psalms is simple: the Lord reigns. And the Psalms are ultimately psalms about life in God's kingdom. First we will discover how this message is communicated in Psalm 2; then we will see how the message of Psalm 2 is the message of the Psalms as a whole.

The Message of Psalm 2

Psalm 2 teaches two dimensions of the Lord's reign, or two ways in which the Lord reigns over his people and over the world.

The Lord Reigns as the Enthroned One

Verse 4 refers to the Lord as "the One enthroned in heaven." The Hebrew word translated "enthroned" is *yashav*, which ordinarily means "sit." Words are interesting. Take the Hebrew word *bayit*, for example. It is often translated "house." If a common person lives in a *bayit*, we call it a house. If God lives in the *bayit*, we call it a temple. And if a king lives in a *bayit*, it is a palace. One word in Hebrew is translated three different ways in English, depending on the context.

So too with the word *yashav*. When the word is used in reference to an ordinary person, we translate *yashav* with "sit," and when it is used in reference to a king, we say that the king is "enthroned." The reason the New International Version translates *yashav* here as "the One enthroned" is that *yashav* is used in reference to the divine King sitting on his royal throne in heaven.

The Lord Is Enthroned in Heaven

The word *yashav* is used in reference to the Lord's reign in other texts that give us insight into Psalm 2. For example, Psalm 29:10 says,

> The LORD sits enthroned [*yashav*] over the flood;
> The LORD is enthroned [*yashav*] as King forever.

It is "as King" that the Lord sits enthroned. And he sits enthroned "over the flood." The word translated "flood" is *mabbul*, which refers to the celestial water supply that deluged the earth in the days of Noah.[1] To say that the Lord sat enthroned over these celestial waters is to say that the Lord is enthroned in heaven. And so Psalm 2:4 pictures God, sitting on his heavenly throne, reigning as king in heaven.

Of course, since the Lord is enthroned in heaven, as opposed to on the earth, he is the divine King. Psalm 47:8 makes this explicit when it says,

> God reigns over the nations.
> God is seated on his holy throne.

Who is the one enthroned in heaven? Hypothetically it could be an angel, but it is not. The one sitting enthroned in heaven is the true and living God. Similarly Psalm 9:2 says,

> I will be glad and rejoice in you.
> I will sing praise to your name, O Most High.

And verse 7 adds,

> The LORD reigns forever;
> he has established his throne in heaven for judgment.

It is the "Most High" God who "reigns forever" from "his throne in heaven." Psalm 2 paints the same picture of the Lord as "the One enthroned in heaven." Psalm 2 also teaches that the Lord is enthroned over the earth as well as in heaven.

The Lord Is Enthroned over the Earth

The psalmist was well aware of the fact that there were human kings ruling on the earth in his day. The psalmist refers to these kings in verse 2:

> The kings of the earth take their stand
> and the rulers gather together.

And he addresses them in verse 10 saying,

> Therefore, you kings, be wise;
> be warned, you rulers of the earth.

God is not the only king. There are human kings. But as the one who is enthroned in heaven, God is the one who is enthroned over the earth: he reigns over all human kings. The Lord is the sovereign King. That is to say, the Lord is the King who is in ultimate control over the affairs of this earth.

This ultimate control is what the human kings desire. They want absolute power. This desire is indicated by their saying, "Let us break their chains . . . and throw off their fetters" (v. 3). We see that the kings, as representative of all humans on the earth, have a misunderstanding of the authority of God. They view God's position of ultimate authority as "chains" and "fetters." People have often thought that living under God's authority would restrict them and hinder them from reaching their full potential. They have not understood that the Lord is good and the exercise of his authority is therefore good and for their good. They have not understood that the truth of God sets people free to be all that God has created them to be (John 8:32). They have not understood the truth that God's law is instruction that brings true freedom (James 1:25) and ultimate well-being (Pss. 1; 112). So rather than submitting to the Lord's authority, they have rebelled against it and sought ultimate authority for themselves.

How does God respond when they say, "Let us break their chains . . . and throw off their fetters"? God responds in a fourfold progression. Recall the progression in Psalm 1 from walking to standing to sitting. There's a similar progression here. The Lord's response begins with laughter. I saw a picture of this one Sunday when we had friends over for the afternoon. While the kids were swimming in the pool, one young boy about four and one-half feet tall was trying to push my sixteen-year-old son into the pool. My son was leaning against a post, chuckling. It didn't take any effort at all for him to ward off the onslaught of his little opponent. In a similar way the Lord laughs at those who try to rebel against his authority in their lives. But then the laugher changes to scoffing, and the scoffing deepens to a rebuke, which is followed by words that strike terror into human hearts. People resist the reign of God to their detriment. Resisting God's authority is the path to death, while living under God's authority brings blessing and life.

Whether people submit or resist does not affect the reality of God's reign. The Lord reigns as the One enthroned in heaven and over all the earth regardless of how humans respond.

The Lord Reigns Through His Anointed One

Sometimes God acts directly in the affairs of the world, and sometimes God acts indirectly. At times he heals without the aid of a doctor, and at other times he heals through the agency of a health practitioner. It seems to me that God ordinarily acts indirectly in our world. I once met a man who became a Christian on his own by reading the Bible. Most Christians, however, came to believe through the witness of another person—a friend, a parent, a preacher. So while it is true that the Lord reigns in heaven and over all the earth, he reigns through human beings. He reigns through his "Anointed One," in the language of Psalm 2.

Through His Messiah

Psalm 2:2 refers to the Lord's Anointed One:

> The kings of the earth take their stand
>   and the rulers gather together

> against the Lord
>   and against his Anointed One.

The Hebrew word translated "Anointed One" is *mashiach*. The English word *messiah* comes from *mashiach*.

A messiah in the Old Testament was someone who had oil poured on him in order to set him apart for a special function. Prophets, priests, and kings were anointed (Exod. 28:41; 1 Kings 1:34; 1 Kings 19:16). In Psalm 2 the Anointed One is the king, as is most frequently the case in the Old Testament and as verse 6 makes clear:

> I have installed my King
>   on Zion, my holy hill.

Anointing with oil was symbolic of the outpouring of the Spirit of God on the king to empower him for his duties. Anointing and the coming of the Spirit are explicitly connected in David's anointing by Samuel.

> So Samuel took the horn of oil and anointed him in the presence of his brothers, and from that day on the Spirit of the Lord came upon David in power. (1 Sam. 16:13)

This empowerment for office could be lost because of sin in the king's life, as was the case with Saul.

> Now the Spirit of the Lord had departed from Saul, and an evil spirit from the Lord tormented him. (1 Sam. 16:14)

After his sin with Bathsheba, David prayed in Psalm 51:11 for the Lord not to take the Holy Spirit from him.

Do not cast me from your presence
  or take your Holy Spirit from me.

David did not want to lose his anointing, the empowerment of the Spirit to carry out his calling as king.

The reign of the Lord and the reign of the anointed king, the messiah, are closely connected in Psalm 2. The opposition of the kings of the nations is simultaneously against the Lord and against his Anointed One (v. 2). The kings want to break "*their* chains" and "*their* fetters"; thus these kings identify the authority of the Lord and the authority of the Anointed One (v. 3). And the messianic king is the one who rules the nations (v. 9).

So while the Lord reigns in heaven and over all the earth, his reign is indirect. His reign is carried out through the agency of his anointed, messianic king—the human king empowered by the divine Spirit to reign over the nations of the earth.

Through David and His Descendants

From David's day on, the Lord reigning through his messianic king meant the Lord reigning through David and his descendants.

Though Psalm 2 does not have a title with information about who the author was, the New Testament identifies David as the author.

> You spoke by the Holy Spirit through the mouth of your servant, our father David:
>
> "Why do the nations rage
>   and the peoples plot in vain?" (Acts 4:25)

Psalm 2 was originally a hymn written for David's coronation as king. Perhaps at some point in the ceremony a priest, speaking for God, would have said,

I have installed my King
  on Zion, my holy hill. (v. 6)

In response David may have said, "I will proclaim the decree of the LORD" (v. 7a) and then gone on to proclaim the promises that God gave him at his coronation as king.

He said to me, "You are my Son;
  today I have become your Father.
Ask of me,
  and I will make the nations your inheritance,
  the ends of the earth your possession.
You will rule them with an iron scepter;
  you will dash them to pieces like pottery." (vv. 7b–9)

The day of coronation was the day of sonship. When David was crowned king, he became son of God in a very special sense. He had a special relationship with the Lord, like that of a son to a father. At the heart of this relationship was David's calling to be the person through whom the Lord would exercise his reign over the nations of the earth. On the day of his coronation, David became the anointed, messianic son of God. And on that day David began to inherit the nations and to rule over them.

While we cannot be sure, it is likely that Psalm 2 would have been used in the subsequent anointings of each of David's descendants who reigned in his place on the throne in Jerusalem. This throne was at the same time the throne of David and the throne of the Lord, as demonstrated by a comparison of the parallel texts 1 Kings 2:12 and 1 Chronicles 29:23.

> So Solomon sat on *the throne of his father David*, and his rule was firmly established. (1 Kings 2:12)

> So Solomon sat on *the throne of the* LORD as king in place of his father David. He prospered and all Israel obeyed him. (1 Chron. 29:23)

David and his sons were the messianic kings empowered by the Holy Spirit to reign over the nations as the human representatives of the divine King of heaven and earth.

Through David's Greater Son

The New Testament identifies Jesus as the ultimate messianic King. For example, John 1:41 records that having encountered Jesus,

> The first thing Andrew did was to find his brother Simon and tell him, "We have found the Messiah" (that is, the Christ).

Like Hebrew *mashiach*, Greek *christos* (translated "Christ") means "anointed." In the face of Jesus, Andrew saw the Anointed One, the Christ, the Messiah, David's greater son (Matt. 22:41–46).

Luke also saw in Jesus' experience the raging of the nations against the Lord and his Anointed One. In Acts 4:23–27 we read,

> On their release, Peter and John went back to their own people and reported all that the chief priests and elders had said to them. When they heard this, they raised

> their voices together in prayer to God. "Sovereign Lord," they said, "you made the heaven and the earth and the sea, and everything in them. You spoke by the Holy Spirit through the mouth of your servant, our father David:
>
> " 'Why do the nations rage
> and the peoples plot in vain?
> The kings of the earth take their stand
> and the rulers gather together
> against the Lord
> and against his Anointed One.'
>
> "Indeed Herod and Pontius Pilate met together with the Gentiles and the people of Israel in this city to conspire against your holy servant Jesus, whom you anointed."

The nations of Psalm 2 are said to be Herod, Pontius Pilate, the Gentiles, and the people of Israel. These Gentiles and Jews "met together." The Greek word translated "met together" is the exact word that is used in the ancient Greek translation of Psalm 2:2, where the New International Version has "gathered together." They "met together" to plot against Jesus, whom Luke identifies as the one whom God had "anointed."

One question that arises is What day was Jesus' coronation day? To put it another way: When did Jesus become Son of God? As to his deity, the Son of God always was—he is the eternal second person of the Trinity. Here, however, we are speaking of Jesus in his incarnation, Jesus as God who became a man, Jesus in his special calling as Messiah. When did Jesus become the messianic Son of God? Not at his birth. Not at his baptism. Not at his crucifixion. Not at his ascension. The New Testament affirms that Jesus became the messianic Son of God at his resurrection from the dead.

Acts 13:28–33 says in reference to Jesus,

> Though they found no proper ground for a death sentence, they asked Pilate to have him executed. When they had carried out all that was written about him, they took him down from the tree and laid him in a tomb. But God raised him from the dead, and for many days he was seen by those who had traveled with him from Galilee to Jerusalem. They are now his witnesses to our people.
>
> We tell you the good news: What God promised our fathers he has fulfilled for us, their children, by raising up Jesus. As it is written in the second Psalm:
>
> "You are my Son;
> today I have become your Father."

Psalm 2 is fulfilled in Jesus. The "today" when Jesus became the Father's Son was the day when the Father raised the Son from the dead. Through his resurrection from the dead Jesus entered into a new phase of his messianic sonship. Through his resurrection the Son in humiliation became the Son in exaltation.

Earlier, in Acts 2:36, Peter assured his fellow Jews that "God has made this Jesus, whom you crucified, both Lord and Christ." God made Jesus something that at least in some sense he was not previously: God made Jesus Lord and Messiah. And according to the previous two verses, this new lordship and messiahship was connected with Jesus exercising his royal dominion over those who had previously opposed him:

For David did not ascend to heaven, and yet he said,

> "The Lord said to my Lord:
> Sit at my right hand
> until I make your enemies
> a footstool for your feet."

Two other texts will help us understand this new lordship and messiahship better.

The first is Romans 1:1–3. Paul opens his letter to the Romans with these words:

> Paul, a servant of Christ Jesus, called to be an apostle and set apart for the gospel of God—the gospel he promised beforehand through his prophets in the Holy Scriptures regarding his Son, who as to his human nature was a descendant of David, and who through the Spirit of holiness was declared with power to be the Son of God by his resurrection from the dead: Jesus Christ our Lord.

Through the agency of the Holy Spirit, Jesus' resurrection from the dead declared that Jesus is the Son of God. The New International Version says this declaration was made "with power." The natural reading of the Greek text, however, leads to the conclusion that "with power" does not describe the Spirit's declaration but amplifies the nature of Jesus' sonship. I think Paul is saying that Jesus' resurrection declared him to be the "Son of God with power."

Jesus exercised great power during his ministry before his death and resurrection. You need only to skim one of the Gospels to see this. So how could he become Son of God with power at his resurrection? Jesus became Son of God in a new sense. He became Son of God with new power.

This brings us to the second text, Matthew 28:18–19. Not before but after his resurrection, Jesus said to his disciples,

> All authority in heaven and on earth has been given to me. Therefore go and make disciples of all nations, baptizing them in the name of the Father and of the Son and of the Holy Spirit.

This seems to mean that after his resurrection God the Father endowed Jesus the Son with a level of authority that he did not possess before the resurrection. And this new level of authority—"all authority in heaven and on earth"—is connected with Jesus commissioning his disciples to go and make disciples of "all nations."

Just as David's coronation day—when he became son of God—was the day he began to extend his reign over the nations, so Jesus' coronation day—when he became Son of God with power—was the day he began to extend his dominion over the nations. Before the resurrection the Good News was preached primarily to one nation, Israel. After the resurrection, the Good News goes to all the nations of the earth over which Jesus has all authority as Son of God with power.

Psalm 2 teaches us that the Lord reigns in heaven and over all the earth and that he reigns though the agency of the messianic Son of God—David, his sons, and his greater Son. I wonder if the rest of the Book of Psalms focuses in some way on the messianic King? Let's turn to the Psalms as a whole and see what we can discover.

THE MESSAGE OF THE BOOK OF PSALMS

We will now discover that we can read the Psalms as a story about the Lord's reign through his messianic King. Let's take a trip through the Book of Psalms.

As a novel is divided into chapters, so the Book of Psalms is divided into five sections, usually referred to as books (Ps. 1–41; 42–72; 73–89; 90–106; 107–150). As you might read the beginning and end of a novel to get the big picture, we will look at the psalms that are at the beginning or end of the various books to get the big picture of the overall message of the Book of Psalms.

For a number of reasons we can divide the Psalms into two large sections, books 1–3 and books 4–5. By the end of book 3 we will be on the edge of our seats as the dramatic tension of the Psalms reaches its climax. Books 4–5 will resolve this tension in three specific ways, two of which we will study in this chapter, the other being the subject of chapter 6.

The Messianic King Is Absent

Though we do not usually think of the Psalms as a narrative, dramatic tension builds in the Psalms as much as in the best novel. Psalm 2 teaches us to expect a story about the successful reign of the Lord through his messianic king. But by the time we get to the end of book 3 we discover that there is no messianic king reigning over Israel, let alone reigning over all the nations of the earth. How could such a grand beginning come to such a low point? Let's find out.

Messianic Kingship Inaugurated and Confirmed

By studying Psalm 2 we have already learned that book 1 begins with the inauguration of the messianic kingship at the time of David's coronation. Psalm 41 brings book 1 to a close by confirming that the plan for the messianic kingship initiated in Psalm 2 is working out perfectly.

Notice how Psalm 41 opens with the word *blessed*. This is the same word that opened Psalm 1. The repetition of "blessed" at the beginning of Psalms 1 and 41 marks the beginning and ending of book 1 in keeping with ancient literary style. The "blessed" person of Psalms 1 and 41 is first and foremost David, as is indicated by the fact the Psalm 41 is "a psalm of David," according to the title.

David is "he who has regard for the weak" (v. 1). And in verse 11 David says, "I know that you are pleased with me." The Hebrew word translated "pleased" is *chafayts*, the same word translated "delights" in Psalm 1:2: "He delights in the law of the LORD." The point seems to be that since David has delighted (*chafayts*) in the Lord's instruction, the Lord delights (*chafayts*) in David.

But how does David know that the Lord delights in him? The next poetic phrase answers this question for us: "for my enemy does not triumph over me." The Lord had promised David that the kings who were raging against him would not prevail over him, and David here testifies to the fulfillment of this promise in his experience. By the end of book 1 the promises made at the inauguration of the messianic kingship have been confirmed. The messianic king is reigning over the nations.

Messianic Kingship Transferred

Who would be the next king after David? Kingship was a new institution in Israel. David was only the second king to reign over Israel. The first king, Saul, was not succeeded by a family member. Would a member of David's family be the next king, and if so, which one? The Lord made a covenant, an agreement with David that one of his sons would succeed him. You can read about this in 2 Samuel 7. As the time of David's death draws near, political intrigue takes center stage when David's son Adonijah sets himself up as king in place of David (1 Kings 1:1–10). But Nathan the prophet and David's wife Bathsheba intervene and have David make Bathsheba's son Solomon king of Israel (1 Kings 1:11–40). Adonijah, out of fear for his life, acknowledges that Solomon is king, and the messianic kingship is transferred from David to Solomon (1 Kings 1:41–53). The end of book 2 affirms this transfer of the messianic kingship from David to Solomon.

The last psalm in book 2 (Ps. 72) is a prayer for "the king," "the royal son" (v. 1). Amazingly, the title to this final psalm is "Of Solomon." Added to this is the remarkable way in which Psalm 72 echoes three key psalms from books 1 and 2: Psalms 1, 2, and 41.

As David had "regard for the weak" in Psalm 41:1, so in Psalm 72 the prayer is for Solomon to "defend the afflicted" and "save the children of the needy" (v. 4). Solomon is the new David. The royal responsibility to care for the needy has been effectively transferred from David to Solomon (see also vv. 12–14).

Verses 8–10 paint a beautiful portrait of Solomon ruling over the nations of the earth "from sea to sea and from the River to the ends of the earth" with his former enemies bowing before him and the once raging kings now bringing him tribute. This portrait casts the description of the messianic king of Psalm 2 before our mind's eye. Not just the kings but also the nations will accept the invitation of Psalm 2 to "serve [*avad*] the LORD," as Psalm 72:11 says:

All kings will bow down to him
and all nations will serve [*avad*] him.

The position of messianic king, called "royal son" (Ps. 72:1) and "my Son" (Ps. 2:7), has been effectively transferred from David to Solomon.

Prosperity characterizes the reign of this king.

The mountains will bring prosperity to the people,
the hills the fruit of righteousness. (v. 3)

He will be like rain falling on a mown field,
like showers watering the earth.
In his days the righteous will flourish;
prosperity will abound till the moon is no more.
(vv. 6–7)

Let grain abound throughout the land;
on the tops of the hills may it sway.
Let its fruit flourish like Lebanon;
let it thrive like the grass of the field. (vv. 16–17)

Notice how this prosperity is portrayed with images drawn consistently from the world of vegetation. This imagery draws us back to Psalm 1, where those who live in keeping with God's instruction are said to be "like a tree planted by streams of water, which yields its fruit in season and whose leaf does not wither"—an image drawn from the world of vegetation. While Psalm 1 has all people in view who live in keeping with God's instruction, one "man" is in view in particular. This "man" of Psalm 1 is the "Son" of Psalm 2. The person primarily in view in Psalm 1 is the messianic king of Psalm 2.[2] In the beginning David is the blessed "man" of Psalm 1, but by the time we reach the end of book 2 the "man" who can be compared with verdant vegetation is Solomon. The messianic kingship has been effectively transferred from David to his son Solomon.

Isn't this wonderful? The messianic kingship inaugurated and confirmed in book 1 has been transferred to the next generation in book 2. What new heights will we scale in book 3?

Messianic Kingship Aborted?

Instead of scaling new heights, book 3 brings us to the depths of despair.

The next to the last psalm in book 3 is Psalm 88. Of all the psalms, Psalm 88 is unquestionably the darkest. With unrelenting anguish the psalmist recounts the depths of despair, as in verse 6, where he says of the Lord,

> You have put me in the lowest pit,
> in the darkest depths.

This darkness hangs like a pall to the last verse of the psalm, which ends with these bleak words, "The darkness is my closest friend." The darkness of Psalm 88 sets the mood for our reading of the final psalm of book 3, Psalm 89.

We are not surprised to discover that Psalm 89 focuses on the messianic kingship inaugurated with David and promised to his sons (vv. 3–4).

> You said, "I have made a covenant with my chosen one,
> I have sworn to David my servant,
> 'I will establish your line forever
> and make your throne firm through all generations.' "

Verses 19–29 echo many of the key themes of Psalm 2. David is "anointed" (v. 20). He will rule over those who stand in opposition to him (vv. 21–25). As the "firstborn," he calls the Lord his God "Father." While it is true that some of David's sons might not experience all of the blessings of kingship because of their disobedience (vv. 30–32), it is equally true that the Davidic dynasty will never come to an end (vv. 33–37).

> I will not take my love from him,
> nor will I ever betray my faithfulness.
> I will not violate my covenant
> or alter what my lips have uttered.
> Once for all, I have sworn by my holiness—
> and I will not lie to David—
> that his line will continue forever
> and his throne endure before me like the sun;
> it will be established forever like the moon,
> the faithful witness in the sky.

Immediately after the reiteration of these glorious promises comes that awful word *but* (vv. 38–39)—that word that seems to negate all that has been said to this point.

> But you have rejected, you have spurned,
> you have been very angry with your anointed one.
> You have renounced the covenant with your servant
> and have defiled his crown in the dust.

Although they were originally written at an earlier time, the words of verses 40–45 take on new depths of despair when they are read against the backdrop of the Babylonian exile.

You have broken through all his walls
 and reduced his strongholds to ruins.
All who pass by have plundered him;
 he has become the scorn of his neighbors.
You have exalted the right hand of his foes;
 you have made all his enemies rejoice.
You have turned back the edge of his sword
 and have not supported him in battle.
You have put an end to his splendor
 and cast his throne to the ground.
You have cut short the days of his youth;
 you have covered him with a mantle of shame.

When the average Israelite looked around in postexilic Judah, a son of David sitting on the throne and ruling over the nations was nowhere to be found. No son of David ruled over the small clan of Judah, let alone all the nations of the earth. One of the most painful and agonizing questions in the hearts of God's people at that time comes to expression in verse 49.

O Lord, where is your former great love,
 which in your faithfulness you swore to David?

What a radical question! The apparent failure of the Davidic monarchy called into question the faithfulness of God. The psalmist voices this radical question as a representative of all the people. For them reading about the faithfulness of God in their Scriptures was not enough. Their faith led them to expect an experience of this faithfulness in the details of their lives. When they did not, radical honesty characterized their speech to God. Here the Holy Spirit leads us to pray with this same kind of honesty when we are not experiencing in our lives the truth that is taught in the Scriptures.

And so Psalm 89 brings the first half of the Book of Psalms to a conclusion with a question that seems to affirm the abortion of the messianic kingship in the absence of a son of David reigning over the nations. The kingship inaugurated and confirmed in book 1 and effectively transferred in book 2 has seemingly come to an end in book 3—and with it the faithfulness of God.

HOW TO LIVE IN THE ABSENCE OF THE MESSIANIC KING

Since the psalms are a manual for abundant living, we would expect books 4 and 5 to provide instruction that responds to the crisis at the end of book 3—instruction on how to live abundantly even though there is no messianic king ruling the nation or nations. Books 4 and 5 give us that instruction, with each book having its own focus.

How do you live with the tension that at times exists between what God's Word says and what you experience in life? These two things don't always line up for a variety of reasons. And the Psalms teach us three principles for abundant living.

Live with Faith

Book 4 teaches the first principle: Live with faith that the Lord reigns in spite of the evidence around you.

The absence of a messianic king seemed to evidence a lack of power on God's part. That Judah was a small part of the large world empire of Persia seemed to say that the God of Judah did not have the power to keep the promises he had made to David and his descendents. Life often appears to contradict the teaching of the Bible that the Lord reigns. How do we live in this tension? We live by faith that the Lord reigns in spite of evidence to the contrary. Let's find out how book 4 teaches us this.

The first words of book 4, the title of Psalm 90, strike us: "A prayer of Moses the man of God." After the excruciating question in Psalm 89, "O LORD, where is your former great love, which in your faithfulness you swore to David?" (v. 45) we encounter a psalm by Moses, who lived some 450 years before David. In fact, the whole of book 4 has a decidedly Mosaic cast to it, since six of the seven uses of "Moses" in the Psalms are in book 4.[3] What is the significance?

Book 4 takes us back before David, before the days of the messianic kingship. And what were those days like? Where did people find their security before there was a king? The opening line of the psalm answers this question for us.

> Lord, you have been our dwelling place
> throughout all generations.

In those days people could live abundantly and securely because God was their king and their security. This was true even before Moses. It has been true from all eternity past that God is God and therefore the ultimate source of security. The faith in God that empowered people for abundant living from before David could still empower people for abundant living in the absence of the messianic king, because the same God was still there. This same faith—that the Lord reigns—empowers us to live abundantly even when there is evidence to the contrary in our lives.

Now let's turn our attention to a cluster of psalms in book 4 that brings us to the heart of the Psalms, Psalms 93–99. Note the sustained emphasis on the reign of God in the world.

The LORD *reigns*, he is robed in majesty;
the LORD is robed in majesty
and is armed with strength.
The world is firmly established;
it cannot be moved. (Ps. 93:1)

For the LORD is the great God,
the great *King* above all gods. (Ps. 95:3)

Say among the nations, "The LORD *reigns*."
The world is firmly established, it cannot be moved.
(Ps. 96:10)

The LORD *reigns*, let the earth be glad;
let the distant shores rejoice. (Ps. 97:1)

Shout for joy before the LORD, the *King*. (Ps. 98:6)

The LORD *reigns*,
let the nations tremble. (Ps. 99:1)

Do you see how book 4 responds to the question raised in Psalm 89? Book 4 responds with a sustained emphasis on the truth the God is still King and God still reigns over the world that he has made. No other group of psalms anywhere in the Book of Psalms contains this sustained emphasis on the kingship of God. This cluster of psalms that follows Psalm 89 teaches us to live by faith that God reigns, even when all of the evidence of life appears to contradict that truth. The truth stands. The Lord reigns. We live by faith.

Live with Obedience

Book 5 teaches the second principle: Live with obedience to the Lord who reigns.

The call to faith continues in book 5. Faith in the Lord is a key theme running through the psalms of ascent, Psalms 120–134.

> I lift up my eyes to the hills—
> where does my help come from?
> My help comes from the LORD,
> the Maker of heaven and earth. (Ps. 121:1)

> I lift up my eyes to you,
> to you whose throne is in heaven. (Ps. 123:1)

> Our help is in the name of the LORD,
> the Maker of heaven and earth. (Ps. 124:8)

> Those who trust in the LORD are like Mount Zion,
> which cannot be shaken but endures forever. (Ps. 125:1)

> Unless the LORD builds the house,
> its builders labor in vain.
> Unless the LORD watches over the city,
> the watchmen stand guard in vain. (Ps. 127:1)

> I wait for the LORD, my soul waits,
> and in his word I put my hope. (Ps. 130:5)

> O Israel, put your hope in the LORD
> both now and forevermore. (Ps. 131:3)

This group of psalms with its focus on faith follows immediately upon the obvious centerpiece of book 5, Psalm 119. And the key word of Psalm 119 is *torah* ("instruction"). The word *torah* occurs twenty-five times in this psalm, and related words occur in 174 of the 176 verses. The theme of this psalm is God's instruction, and in a variety of ways the psalmist encourages us to live in keeping with this instruction. We are to "walk" according to it (v. 1), "keep" it (vv. 34, 44, 55), not "turn from" it (v. 51), and not "forget" it (vv. 61, 109, 153). All this is to say we are to live with obedience to God's instruction as part of the path of abundant living.

What kind of obedience are we talking about? Given the focus on faith in Psalm 120–134, we are not talking about a legalistic obedience. True obedience arises naturally out of a living faith in the Lord who reigns. And there is more. There are two key qualifiers of our obedience to the Lord's instruction. One comes from Psalm 119, and the other comes from the grand doxology at the end of book 5.

An Obedience of Love. First, our obedience is an obedience of love. Perhaps verse 97 captures the heart of Psalm 119 better than any other verse.

> Oh, how I love your law,
> I meditate on it all day long.

In verses 113 and 163 the psalmist says, "I love your law." And in verse 165 we receive this wonderful promise:

> Great peace have they who love your law,
> and nothing can make them stumble.

Our obedience does not simply come from the will; it is not bare duty. Our obedience wells up from a heart that loves God because of who he is and all that he has done for us.

Since we love God, we love God's instruction, which delights us (see vv. 70, 77, 92, 174) and does not burden us. We love God's instruction for a variety of reasons, and one is that by living in keeping with this instruction from a heart of love we experience "peace," as the psalmist says in verse 165. This "peace" is Hebrew *shalom*, which is similar in meaning to "blessed" in Psalm 1. Interestingly enough, Psalm 119 begins with "blessed."[4]

> Blessed are they whose ways are blameless,
> who walk according to the law of the LORD. (v. 1)

We love God's instruction because it is the path of life, abundant life.

> Your statutes are forever right;
> give me understanding that I may live. (Ps. 119:144)

An Obedience of Worship. Second, our obedience is an obedience of worship.

Psalm 145 is a psalm of praise. This is the one time where the word *praise*, used in the ancient Hebrew title of the Book of Psalms, is used in the title of a specific psalm: "A Psalm of Praise. Of David." Although the people of God in the days after the Babylonian exile did not have a son of David reigning over them and the nations, they did have a reconstructed version of the temple built by David's son Solomon. And they did have David's example, as recorded in Psalm 145.

I will exalt you, my God the King;
  I will praise your name for ever and ever.
Every day I will praise you
  and extol your name for ever and ever.

Two things strike us. First, David confesses that God is his King. If God is the king's King, then God is the ultimate King. Though there may not have been a messianic king, the ultimate and divine King was still on the scene and still reigning over the nations of the earth. So the people of God could follow David's example by trusting in the divine King to rule over them. Second, a core component of David's reason for being was the worship of God. David lived to worship. He tells us that his "mouth will speak in praise of the LORD" (v. 21). Psalms 146–150, where the praise of God dominates, can be viewed as the kind of words that filled David's mouth and that can fill our lives as well.

Worship, in public and in private, is a focal point of our life of obedience to God. For in worship we come humbly, gratefully, and joyfully to praise the ultimate source of all life. And all of life is now worship, as living in keeping with God's instruction is our response to the greatness of who he is and what he has done for us (Rom. 12:1–2).

The abundant life is a life of faith in the Lord who reigns even when all evidence points us in another direction. And this faith is a living faith that lives in keeping with God's instructions. This obedience has its origin in love and its goal in worship.

But is that all to our response? Do we trust and obey and then accept the lack of evidence for the reign of God in our lives as the way things are and always will be? Or is there yet one more principle for living abundantly in the absence of evidence for the Lord's reign?

The third principle is that we live with hope that the King will come into the reality of our lives and bring the salvation that results in abundant life. This hope permeates the Psalms and will occupy our minds and fill our hearts in the next chapter.

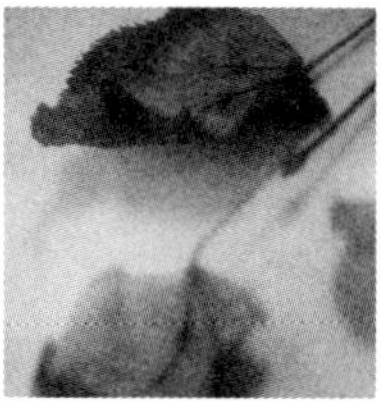

6

Blessed Is He Who Comes

The Psalms and the Future

Give thanks to the LORD, for he is good;
his love endures forever.

. . . .

I will give you thanks, for you answered me;
you have become my salvation.

The stone the builders rejected
has become the capstone;
the LORD has done this,
and it is marvelous in our eyes.
This is the day the LORD has made;
let us rejoice and be glad in it.

O LORD, save us;
O LORD, grant us success.

Blessed is he who comes in the name of the LORD.
From the house of the LORD *we bless you.*

. . . .

You are my God, *and I will give you thanks;*
you are my God, *and I will exalt you.*

Give thanks to the LORD, *for he is good;*
his love endures forever.
(Ps. 118:1, 21–26, 28–29)

In the last chapter we learned that the Book of Psalms was compiled in part to teach the original readers how to live in the absence of the messianic king. The Psalms taught them to live with faith in the truth that the Lord reigns in spite of evidence to the contrary. And this faith was to be a living faith that obeys out of love and in worship. But is there more?

Do the Psalms teach more about how to live in the absence of the messianic king? More than living by faith and obedience, as important as these are? Yes! There is more, and this "more" comes to expression in texts like Psalm 118.

The title of this chapter is taken from Psalm 118:26: "Blessed is he who comes in the name of the LORD." In this chapter we will discover that in addition to teaching us to live with faith that the Lord reigns in spite of evidence to the contrary, the Psalms also teach us to live with hope, with hope that the King is coming.

We can say that the whole Book of Psalms is eschatological. This means, among other things, that the Book of Psalms was driving the original audience forward. One purpose of the Psalms was and is to create a sense of hope that one day the King would come to put everything in our lives and in the world in right order once and for all.

We're going to find out that the Psalms create an expectation that the King is coming in two senses. In one sense the expectation is that the King who is coming is the Lord. In another sense the King who is coming is the Messiah. Let's see where and how the Psalms create this hope.

The King Is Coming: He Is the Lord

In one sense the Lord has always been King over all that he has made. The Psalms also teach that the Lord becomes King in a complementary sense. This latter sense provides the foundation for the hope that the King will come in the future to establish his reign in a new and fuller way.

The Lord Is King

In the previous chapter we learned that the central message of the Psalms is that the Lord reigns or that the Lord is King. Now we can add more detail to that affirmation, as we discover that the Lord reigns in an eternal kingship and a coming kingship.

An Eternal Kingship

The Book of Psalms celebrates the eternal kingship of the Lord. Take Psalm 93:1–2, for example.

> The LORD reigns, he is robed in majesty;
> the LORD is robed in majesty
> and is armed with strength.
> The world is firmly established;
> it cannot be moved.
> Your throne was established long ago;
> you are from all eternity.

Our knowledge of how Hebrew poetry works helps us to conclude quite easily that the Lord has been King from all eternity. The first colon of the last line affirms that the Lord's "throne was established long ago." Just how long ago? The second colon answers this question: "You are from eternity." Were this poetic line written in Hebrew prose, it would translate into English as "LORD, your reign was established a long time ago; in fact, just as you have always existed, so has your kingship." The Lord's kingship is eternal.

A Coming Kingship

While it is true that the Lord has always been King, the Psalms teach a complementary truth: The Lord becomes King in a new and fuller way.

How the Lord Becomes King. The Hebrew phrase that the New International Version translates "the LORD reigns" in Psalm 93:1 is *YHWH malach*. For some time scholars have debated how best to translate this phrase, which also occurs in Psalms 96:10, 97:1, and 99:1; the related phrase, "God reigns," occurs in Psalm 47:8. All major English translations agree with the New International Version and use a present tense. This is a bit odd, since the verb form in Hebrew is elsewhere typically translated with a past tense (e.g., "has become king" or "was king" or "reigned"). Here are two examples.

> Go in to King David and say to him, "My lord the king, did you not swear to me your servant: 'Surely Solomon your son shall be king after me, and he will sit on my throne'? Why then *has* Adonijah *become king* [*malach*]?" (1 Kings 1:13)

> Rehoboam son of Solomon *was king* [*malach*] in Judah. He was forty-one years old when he became king, and he *reigned* [*malach*] seventeen years in Jerusalem. (1 Kings 14:21)

In addition, the ancient Greek translation of the Hebrew Bible, the Septuagint, consistently translates *YHWH malach* with a past tense that can be used to signal the beginning of a new situation. The truth that the Lord has always been King underlies, I think, the decision to use a present tense in English. Yet there are grammatical and theological reasons for translating *YHWH malach* with "the LORD has become King."

Whether the personal name comes before or after the verb in Hebrew does not matter. Both word orders are used in Hebrew for "has become king."

> Then Absalom sent secret messengers throughout the tribes of Israel to say, "As soon as you hear the sound of the trumpets, then say, 'Absalom is king [verb + name] in Hebron.'" (2 Sam. 15:10)

> Then Nathan asked Bathsheba, Solomon's mother, "Have you not heard that Adonijah, the son of Haggith, has become king [name + verb] without our lord David's knowing it?" (1 Kings 1:11)

Whether or not we translate *YHWH malach* with "is king," as the New International Version does in 2 Samuel 15:10, or with "has become king," as in 1 Kings 1:11, it is clear that *YHWH malach* has an event in view in the immediate past, not a general state of sovereignty. So, for example, when the New International Version translates *malach avshalom* with "Absalom is king" (2 Sam. 15:10), it is still clear that the crowd is proclaiming that Absalom has just now become king.

But how can it be said that the Lord, who has always been king, has now become king? A significant clue is found in the "new song" worshipers are called to sing in psalms that celebrate the Lord's kingship.

> Sing to the LORD a new song;
> sing to the LORD, all the earth. (Ps. 96:1)

Why would a "new song" be sung to the Lord? One reason would be that something new has taken place that calls for celebration. What could this new thing be?

> Sing to the LORD a new song,
> for he has done marvelous things. (Ps. 98:1)

The "new song" is sung when the Lord does something new that is also marvelous. Anytime the Lord does something marvelous a "new song" is appropriate to celebrate the new deed.

> Sing to the LORD a new song,
> for he has done marvelous things;
> his right hand and his holy arm
> have worked salvation for him. (Ps. 98:1)

The "marvelous things" in this text refer to times when the Lord has "worked salvation." When the Lord does something new and marvelous that establishes his reign in a new way, we can say that the Lord has become King in a new way. When the kingdom of

God comes in a new way, God becomes King in a new way. This is, I believe, what is going on in Psalms 93:1, 96:10, 97:1, and 99:1. Are there any particular times when the Lord became King in a new sense?

When the Lord Becomes King. In three key events in the history of the world the Lord becomes king in a new way: consummation, redemption, and creation.

The Lord is going to become King in a new way at the *consummation* of world history.

In Revelation 11:15–17 we read,

> The seventh angel sounded his trumpet, and there were loud voices in heaven, which said:
>
> "The kingdom of the world *has become* the kingdom of our Lord and of his Christ,
> and he will reign for ever and ever."
>
> And the twenty-four elders, who were seated on their thrones before God, fell on their faces and worshiped God, saying:
>
> "We give thanks to you, Lord God Almighty,
> the One who is and who was,
> because you have taken your great power
> and *have begun to reign.*"

Note precisely what the loud voices proclaim: "The kingdom of the world *has become* the kingdom of our Lord and of his Christ." If the kingdom of this world "has become" the kingdom of our Lord and of his Messiah, then at least in some sense the kingdom of this world was not the kingdom of our Lord and his Christ. Something new has taken place in history. The Lord has begun to reign in a new way. This is explicit in the last verse of thanksgiving:

> We give thanks to you, Lord God Almighty,
>   the One who is and who was,
> because you have taken your great power
>   and *have begun to reign*.

The Greek verb translated "have begun to reign" is in the aorist tense, and one use of this tense is to signal the beginning of a new situation. At the consummation of world history the Lord will begin to reign in a fuller way than he is currently reigning, and "he will reign for ever and ever." At present there are still those who rage against him, and all things in this world are not yet running according to God's original design.

When does God become King? He always was King, and he becomes King at the consummation.

The Lord became King in *redemption*. We can begin with the grand redemptive event of the Old Testament, the exodus from Egypt, celebrated in Exodus 15:1–4, 18.

> Then Moses and the Israelites sang this song to the LORD:
>
> > "I will sing to the LORD,
> >   for he is highly exalted.
> > The horse and its rider
> >   he has hurled into the sea.
> > The LORD is my strength and my song;

> he has become my salvation.
> He is my God, and I will praise him,
> my father's God, and I will exalt him.
> The Lord is a warrior;
> the Lord is his name.
> Pharaoh's chariots and his army
> he has hurled into the sea.
> The best of Pharaoh's officers
> are drowned in the Red Sea.
>
> . . . .
>
> The Lord will reign
> for ever and ever."

The people of Israel celebrate the truth that the Lord "*has become* my salvation." The Lord became their salvation when he came as a "mighty warrior" to defeat the Egyptians and to redeem his people. So a new song of redemption is sung to commemorate this event. This event is the beginning of the reign of the Lord in a new way, and, as in Revelation 11:15–17, this new reign will go on "for ever and ever." When the Lord established his dominion in a new way at the time of the exodus, it can be said that he became King in a new way.

In John 12:31–32, Jesus in speaking of his death said,

> Now is the time for judgment on this world; now the prince of this world will be driven out. But I, when I am lifted up from the earth, will draw all men to myself.

Before the grand redemptive event of the New Testament, the crucifixion of Christ, this world had a prince ruling over it. But when Jesus was crucified, the reign of that prince was replaced by the reign of a new King. And this reign of the new King brought with it the salvation of "all men." As "all who take refuge" in the Lord by submitting to his Messiah are "blessed" in Psalm 2:12, so too here the redemptive work of God brings salvation to "all men." The promise in the Psalms that "all" will be blessed is fulfilled in the redemption accomplished by the Lord Jesus Christ. In this redemption the kingdom of God comes in a new way and the Lord becomes King in a new sense.

The Lord becomes King at the consummation because he has previously become King in redemption.

If we go even further back, God became King at *creation*.

When God created the heavens and the earth, he established his kingship in a new way in history. In the mythology of ancient Babylon, kingship and creation were joined. The Babylonian god Marduk established his kingship over the gods by defeating Tiamat, who represented the forces of chaos, and by creating the upper and lower levels of the universe out of her corpse. I mention this to point out that in the world of the ancient Israelites the act of creating the universe and the establishment of divine kingship were related events.

We see this same correlation in Psalm 74:12–15:

> But you, O God, are my king from of old;
> you bring salvation upon the earth.
> It was you who split open the sea by your power;
> you broke the heads of the monster in the waters.
> It was you who crushed the heads of Leviathan
> and gave him as food to the creatures of the desert.
> It was you who opened up springs and streams;
> you dried up the ever flowing rivers.

This text celebrates the Lord's kingship: "But you, O God, are my king from of old." On a first reading of this text, the seemingly obvious reference lying behind God splitting open the sea, breaking the heads of the monster in the waters, crushing the heads of Leviathan, and drying up the ever flowing rivers is the redemption of Israel at the Red Sea. And God being "king from of old" would refer to the establishment of the Lord's reign at the Red Sea. The next verses, however, take us to a time before the crossing of the sea. They take us back to the time of creation.

> The day is yours, and yours also the night;
> you established the sun and moon.
> It was you who set all the boundaries of the earth;
> you made both summer and winter. (Ps. 74:16–17)

The images in the first several verses are metaphorical references to God's work at creation, when he made day and night and established the boundaries of the earth. These images are drawn from the myths of the surrounding cultures, not because Israel held to those myths but because the ancient Israelite poet wanted to say that when God created the heavens and the earth he became King of the cosmos. To teach that God became King at the time of creation the poet used metaphorical language that would have communicated this truth clearly and powerfully to the ancient audience.

Psalm 93:1–4 likewise connects kingship and creation.

> The LORD reigns, he is robed in majesty;
> the LORD is robed in majesty
> and is armed with strength.
> The world is firmly established;
> it cannot be moved.

Your throne was established long ago;
  you are from all eternity.

The seas have lifted up, O LORD,
  the seas have lifted up their voice;
  the seas have lifted up their pounding waves.
Mightier than the thunder of the great waters,
  mightier than the breakers of the sea—
the LORD on high is mighty.

While this psalm affirms the Lord's eternal kingship, as we have already learned, it also affirms that this eternal kingship came into our world in a new way at creation. Just as Tiamat, the forces of chaos, opposed Marduk in the Babylonian myth, the seas, which also represent the forces of chaos, lifted up their voices in opposition to the Lord in Psalm 93. But the Lord proved himself mightier than the chaotic forces of the sea and established the world so that it could not be "moved." This language speaks of God's work of creation here as it does elsewhere in the Old Testament. Take Psalm 104:5, for example:

He set the earth on its foundations;
  it can never be moved.

The Lord became King at the time of creation. The Lord has always been King, and he becomes King in a new sense at creation, in redemption, and ultimately in the consummation.

The Lord Is Coming

Hope stands alongside the idea that the Lord becomes King in a new way by establishing his reign in a new situation to an ever fuller degree—hope that the Lord is coming. Ancient Israel lived with the hope that the Lord would come into their situation and put everything in order for them. This hope bursts into flame in the psalms that celebrate the kingship of God. Psalms 96:13 and 98:9 announce with grand simplicity, "he is coming" (NASB, NRSV), and in context this coming is twofold: the Lord is coming in triumph, and he is coming to judge. Let's look at Psalms 96 and 98 as they express this twofold hope.

The Lord Is Coming in Triumph

While ancient Israel celebrated the marvel that the Lord had just come and accomplished salvation and established his reign in a new sense, they knew that there was still more to come. They knew that everything was not yet right in their lives. They lived with continual hope that the Lord would come again to establish his kingship in deeper dimensions. They lived with hope that the Lord would come to triumph over the forces of chaos that yet remain to be vanquished.

In Psalm 98:1 we read,

> Sing to the LORD a new song,
> for he has done marvelous things;
> his right hand and his holy arm
> have worked salvation for him.

The first line celebrates the truth that the Lord has come and done marvelous thing. What marvelous things has he done? The second lines answers in terms of salvation. In a similar way Psalm 96:1–3 says,

> Sing to the LORD a new song;
> sing to the LORD, all the earth.

Sing to the LORD, praise his name;
  proclaim his salvation day after day.
Declare his glory among the nations,
  his marvelous deeds among all peoples.

God's "salvation," "glory," and "marvelous deeds" all share the same reference, times when the Lord came into the lives of his people to establish his reign by triumphing over the forces that opposed them. Distant acts of salvation, like creation, are in view, as Psalm 96:5, 10 makes clear.

For all the gods of the nations are idols,
  but the LORD made the heavens.

. . . .

Say among the nations, "The LORD reigns."
  The world is firmly established, it cannot be moved.

Creation is also in view in Psalms 93 and 95:1–5. Acts of redemption are also in view, as echoed in Psalm 98:2–3.

The LORD has made his salvation known
  and revealed his righteousness to the nations.
He has remembered his love
  and his faithfulness to the house of Israel;
all the ends of the earth have seen
  the salvation of our God.

These psalms would have been used to celebrate how the Lord had come in specific ways in more recent history, in the experience of those using these psalms at any given time. These psalms could have been used, for example, when the Lord sent rain to triumph over drought or when he came and triumphed over Israel's military enemies. In keeping with this ancient use, we too can celebrate God's coming into our lives, whether that is his coming in his Son to triumph over our sin and guilt or his coming to triumph over illness or poverty or broken relationships. These are examples of God's marvelous deeds of salvation that he has accomplished in our lives. These are examples of the King's coming to triumph over the chaos that remains around us. As God has accomplished and continues to accomplish salvation in large and small ways, he has become and continues to become King in new and more profound ways. What the King has done fills us with hope for what he will do. He is coming, and his coming is in triumph.

The Lord Is Coming to Judge

When the King comes in triumph, he comes to "judge," in the language of Psalms 96:12b–13 and 98:9.

> Then all the trees of the forest will sing for joy;
> they will sing before the LORD, for he comes,
> he comes to judge the earth.
> He will judge the world in righteousness
> and the peoples in his truth.
>
> Let them sing before the LORD,
> for he comes to judge the earth.
> He will judge the world in righteousness
> and the peoples with equity.

Does the word *judge* evoke positive or negative feelings in you? In these psalms the Lord's coming to judge is positive. If this coming to judge were not positive, why would the whole created order being singing?

> Let the heavens rejoice, let the earth be glad;
> let the sea resound, and all that is in it;
> let the fields be jubilant, and everything in them.
> Then all the trees of the forest will sing for joy;
> they will sing before the LORD, for he comes,
> he comes to judge the earth. (Ps. 96:11–13)

To judge (*shafat*) means to put everything in right order. As one author has said, *shafat* "designates an action that restores the disturbed order of a . . . community."[1] While a judge can put things in right order by rendering a verdict in a court of law, it would be a mistake to restrict the meaning of *shafat* to this one idea. The word *shafat* has a much broader use. The heavens rejoice, the sea resounds, the fields are jubilant, the rivers clap their hands, and the trees and mountains sing (Ps. 96:11–12; 98:7–8), not because the Judge is rendering a verdict but because the King is restoring the entire created order.

All things in life are not as God originally intended them to be. This is true for those who first used the Psalms after the return from the Babylonian captivity and for us as well. A quick comparison of Psalms 1:3–4 and 37:7 demonstrates this point. The former says,

> Whatever he does prospers.
>
> Not so the wicked!

This poetic line articulates the right order: those who do what is right succeed and those who don't, don't. But then comes Psalm 37:7.

Be still before the LORD and wait patiently for him;
do not fret when men succeed in their ways,
when they carry out their wicked schemes.

The Hebrew word translated "succeed" is the same word translated "prospers" in Psalm 1:3. Do you feel the tension? Psalm 1 says that those who live out of accord with God's instruction don't succeed, and Psalm 37:7 envisions these same people succeeding. Psalm 37:35 portrays those who violate God's instruction in terms reminiscent of Psalm 1.

I have seen a wicked and ruthless man
flourishing like a green tree in its native soil.

This is not the way things are supposed to be. This is not the right order.

The King is coming to put all things in right order for the whole created realm.

Let them sing before the LORD,
for he comes to judge the earth.
He will judge the world in righteousness
and the peoples with equity. (Ps. 98:9)

Not only will he put all things in right order for "the peoples," but also he will put all things in right order for "the earth," and that means for the entire created realm.

Paul teaches us that the created realm has been "subjected to frustration" and is in "bondage to decay" and is "groaning as in the pains of childbirth right up to the present time" (Rom. 8:18–22). This is not what God originally intended. This is not the way things are supposed to be. This is not the right order. But the creation does not accept this state of affairs as the way things will always be. The creation "waits in eager expectation" and waits "in hope" that God will come and put everything in right order (Rom. 8:19–20).

Psalms 96 and 98 paint a picture of creation celebrating the coming of the King to establish his reign and restore the disturbed order that has too long prevailed over this blighted humanity and the creation. The King who redeems is the King who created, and his redemption is as wide as his creation.

The Book of Psalms is historical. It celebrates the truth that the Lord has come and accomplished salvation in the past. And the Book of Psalms is eschatological. It celebrates the truth that the Lord is coming. He is coming to put everything in right order.

THE KING IS COMING: HE IS THE MESSIAH

In Psalm 2 we learned that the Lord reigns through his Anointed One. The Lord as King reigns through the messianic king. We have also learned that the ancient Israelites went through a tremendous theological crisis after the exile, when the temple was rebuilt but the dynasty of David was not reestablished. In this context books 4–5 can be read as answering this crisis by instructing the people to live with faith that the Lord reigns in spite of evidence to the contrary. Now we have learned that the Psalms also taught the people to live with hope that the Lord would come and put all things in right order. But what about the promise made to David, that he would never fail to have a son sitting on the throne? What about the promise of a messianic king?

The Book of Psalms not only taught the ancient Israelites to live with hope that the Lord would come; it also taught them to live with the expectation that the messianic king would come to reign on the throne of David. Let's discover how by studying Psalm 132 and then Psalm 118.

The Covenant with David Has Not Been Aborted

Psalm 89:49 brought book 3 of the Psalms to a close with the agonizing question, "O Lord, where is your former great love, which in your faithfulness you swore to David?" Psalm 132 adds to the answer we discovered in books 4 and 5. This psalm can be divided into two stanzas. In the first (vv. 1–10) the psalmist makes a plea to the Lord, and the second contains a promise from the Lord.

A Plea to the Lord

The first stanza begins with plea.

> O Lord, remember David
> and all the hardships he endured.

Does this plea come from the lips of someone who has given up all hope that a son of David will rule the nations? This prayer comes from a heart of hope, from a faith that the promise made to David may yet be fulfilled.

The stanza ends with a plea.

> For the sake of David your servant,
> do not reject your anointed one.

David has not disappeared from the hearts of the people in the era after the captivity. Psalm 89:38 seemingly indicates that the Lord had rejected David and his sons once and for all.

> But you have rejected, you have spurned,
> you have been very angry with your anointed one.

But faith rises to new heights in Psalm 132:10, which prays against the seeming hopelessness of Psalm 89:38.

> For the sake of David your servant,
> do not reject your anointed one.

When the eyes of flesh can see no evidence of the promise coming true, the eyes of faith penetrate the darkness and see the light of hope on the horizon. Here the Holy Spirit teaches us to plead when the promise seems to have failed, to hold on to the promise by faith, and when there is no reason to hope, to hope in God.

The plea of Psalm 132 teaches us that in the minds and hearts of God's ancient people the covenant with David had not been aborted. Hope burned in those ancient hearts, at times perhaps like a flickering flame and at times like bright blaze.

A Promise from the Lord

The promise is that the promise stands.

> The LORD swore an oath to David,
> a sure oath that he will not revoke:
> "One of your own descendents
> I will place on your throne. . . ." (Ps. 132:11)

Individual sons may not enjoy the benefits of the promise (v. 12), but the promise is that the promise stands. The apparent failure of the promise (Ps. 89) is not reality. Reality is that the promise stands.

Psalm 132:13–18 tell us several things about Zion/Jerusalem, the first being that the Lord reigns in and from Jerusalem.

> This is my resting place for ever and ever;
> here I will sit enthroned, for I have desired it. (v. 14)

Second, everyone living under the reign of the Lord in Jerusalem will experience an abundant life.

> I will bless her with abundant provisions;
> her poor will I satisfy with food. (v. 15)

Third, the Lord will once again place a son of David on the throne in Jerusalem as his Anointed One.

> Here I will make a horn grow for David
> and set up a lamp for my anointed one. (v. 17)

The promise is that the promise stands. Here the promise comes in the form of two metaphors, a horn and a lamp.

We can understand the metaphor of the lamp from the Book of Kings. In 1 Kings 15:1–3 we read a summary of the reign of Abijah, a son of David who failed to live in keeping with God's instructions.

> In the eighteenth year of the reign of Jeroboam son of Nebat, Abijah became king of Judah, and he reigned in

> Jerusalem three years. His mother's name was Maacah daughter of Abishalom. He committed all the sins his father had done before him; his heart was not fully devoted to the LORD his God, as the heart of David his forefather had been.

Abijah forfeited the benefits of the promise made to David and his sons.

> Nevertheless, for David's sake the LORD his God gave him a lamp in Jerusalem by raising up a son to succeed him and by making Jerusalem strong. (1 Kings 15:4)

"Lamp" is a metaphor for a son who will succeed Abijah as the messianic king, and the lamp is given because the promise made to David will be fulfilled in spite of the errant ways of any particular sons of David. Perhaps the picture is that as a lamp burns throughout the night, David will have a son on the throne throughout the whole of history.

What is the meaning of the metaphor of a "horn"? If you picture two bulls with large horns, battling for supremacy, you will get the point. The horn is a symbol of power. The promise in Deuteronomy 33:17 is that the tribe of Joseph, that is, Ephraim and Manasseh, will be as powerful as a bull.

> In majesty he is like a firstborn bull;
>   his horns are the horns of a wild ox.
> With them he will gore the nations,
>   even those at the ends of the earth.
> Such are the ten thousands of Ephraim;
>   such are the thousands of Manasseh.

The horned bull will rule the nations with great power. To make a horn grow (Ps. 132:17) means to establish a son of David in Jerusalem who will reign with great power like a horned bull.

The Lord here promises to make a horn grow for David. Did he keep his promise? Let's ask Zechariah, a faithful believer at the turn of the era, whether the Lord kept this promise.

At the birth of his son John the Baptist, who was the forerunner of Jesus, Zechariah proclaimed,

> Praise be to the Lord, the God of Israel,
> because he has *come* and has redeemed his people.
> He has raised up a *horn* of salvation for us
> *in the house of his servant David.* (Luke 1:68–69)

Zechariah, and many others in his day, believed that in the coming of the Lord Jesus, the Lord God of Israel had *come*, and that this coming had accomplished redemption; this redemption was accomplished through a *horn from the house of David.* Beyond doubt, Zechariah had Psalm 132:17 in his mind when he uttered these words, and probably Psalm 118:26 was in his mind as well.

Faithful people of God in the postexilic period and beyond took God at his word. They believed the promises: that the Lord was going to come and put all things in right order and that the Son of David was going to come as the agent of this salvation. The Book of Psalms said to the original readers and says to us: "He is coming. You cannot see him with the eyes of flesh, but with the eyes of faith you can see him on the horizon. Live with hope, because the promise is that the promise stands."

The Son of David Is Coming

We can conclude this chapter by returning to our starting point, Psalm 118. Psalm 118 is quoted frequently in the New Testament. Let's look at some of those New Testament quotations to see what the people at the turn of the era were expecting. What hope did Psalm 118 generate in their hearts?

THERE WAS AN EXPECTATION OF "ONE TO COME"

Basing their hope on texts like Psalms 96:13, 98:9, and 118:26, believers lived with an expectation of One to come. This is evident in the life of John the Baptist and his disciples. John the Baptist was a man of great faith, and he was a man who developed some doubts over time. John understood that he was not the Messiah (John 1:20). He knew that he was the one to prepare the way for the coming of the Lord and his Anointed One (John 1:23). He professed that Jesus was "the Lamb of God, who takes away the sin of the world" (John 1:29). Later, however, John sent his disciples to Jesus with this question: "Are you *the one who was to come*, or should we expect someone else?" (Luke 7:20). Why did John move from faith to doubt? What led him to doubt that God had come to establish his reign in a new way through Jesus? The answer is simple. John was in jail.

His thoughts must have been something like this: "If the Lord has come to reign and Jesus is his Anointed One, then why am I in prison? Perhaps Jesus is not the One who is to come." Like John, we can develop doubts when the promises of God are not fulfilled on our timetable or in the way we envisioned.

Nevertheless John's experience serves to teach us that he, like others in his day, was living with the hope that there was One who was to come. They were living with the vital expectation that the messianic king was coming.

He Comes in Triumph

On the first Palm Sunday, Jesus came riding into Jerusalem on a donkey. From our cultural vantage point this might signify that Jesus rode in as a poor man on a beast of burden. Those who lined the road in Jesus' day concluded something quite different. They saw the King riding his royal mount. In 1 Kings 1:33–34 David said,

> Take your lord's servants with you and set Solomon my son on *my own mule* and take him down to Gihon. There have Zadok the priest and Nathan the prophet *anoint him king* over Israel. Blow the trumpet and shout, "Long live King Solomon!"

In keeping with this, Zechariah said,

> Rejoice greatly, O Daughter of Zion!
> Shout, Daughter of Jerusalem!
> See, *your king comes* to you,
> righteous and having salvation,
> gentle and *riding on a donkey*,
> on a colt, the foal of a donkey. (Zech. 9:9)

When they saw their king, they shouted, "Hosanna! Blessed is he who comes in the name of the Lord! Blessed is the King of Israel!" (John 12:13). They understood that Jesus was the King of Israel, the One who was to come and bring salvation. Matthew 21:9 puts it this way, "Hosanna to the Son of David! Blessed is he who comes in the name of the Lord! Hosanna in the highest!" They understood that Jesus was the long-awaited Son of David, the One who was to come and bring salvation. They understood that Jesus was the One who was to come and that he was coming in triumph.

His Triumph Is Through Suffering

But the crowds did not understand that Jesus' triumph was to be through suffering.

Jesus taught this truth, among other places, in the parable of the tenants. After his triumphal entry, Jesus told the story about a landowner who rented out a vineyard to some farmers (Matt. 21:33–41). At harvest time he returned to collect what was owed him. The farmers refused to pay, abusing and even killing the landowner's messengers. Finally he decided to send his son, thinking that the farmers would surely respect the son and pay their dues. Instead they killed the son, thinking that they would then be able to keep the vineyard for themselves. At the conclusion of this story, Jesus quoted Psalm 118:22:

> The stone the builders rejected
> has become the capstone.

Jesus understood that he was the son in the parable and that he was the One who was to come in triumph and that his triumph would be accomplished though being "the stone the builders rejected." He knew that his triumph was to be accomplished on the cross, where he would vanquish the prince of this world, death, and all the forces of chaos that oppose the kingdom of God. His triumph is through suffering.

He Gives a Promise for the Future

But Jesus also knew that the cross was not the end. He knew that the day of resurrection was soon to follow, when he would be declared Son of God with power (Rom. 1:4). Because he knew that chaos and death would be swallowed up in the triumph of resurrection, he gave his disciple a promise for the future in Matthew 23:39:

> I tell you, you will not see me again until you say, "Blessed is he who comes in the name of the Lord."

Just as Psalm 118 gave hope to the ancient people of God, urging them to look forward to the day when the messianic King would come, so Jesus used this psalm to give the same hope to his first disciples and to us.

We live with hope that the King will come into our experiences and drive out the chaos and establish his reign that results in abundant life. We hope for his coming in this life, and we hope for his coming to inaugurate the life to come. And at that time Jesus will put all things in right order. In Revelation 21:3–4 John says,

> I heard a loud voice from the throne saying, "Now the dwelling of God is with men, and he will live with them. They will be his people, and God himself will be with them and be their God. He will wipe every tear from their eyes. There will be no more death or mourning or crying or pain, for the old order of things has passed away."

And at the end of the Book, Jesus says, "Behold, I am coming soon" (Rev. 22:7). He then says, "Blessed is he who keeps the words of the prophecy in this book." When Jesus comes, the blessedness of Psalm 1 comes in all its fullness. So we live with faith that the Lord reigns in spite of all evidence to the contrary. And this faith is a faith that lives in keeping with the Lord's instructions for an abundant life. And we live with hope—hope for more and more of this abundant life now and the fullness of this abundant life at the second coming of the One who said, "I came that they may have life, and have it abundantly" (John 10:10 NASB).

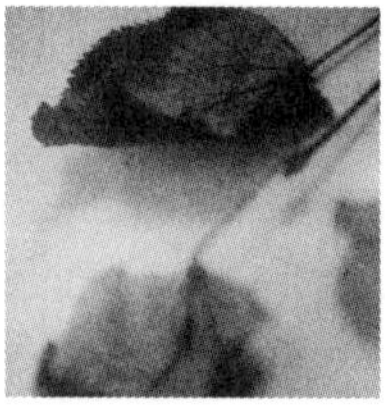

Notes

Chapter 1: Praise the Lord: The Psalms as Praise

1 I have used a simplified system to transliterate Hebrew words throughout this book so that readers can approximate the Hebrew pronunciation.

Chapter 2: Open My Eyes: The Psalms as Poetry

1 Gary Hotham, *Breathmarks: Haiku to Read in the Dark* (Moscow, Ida.: Canon Press, 1999).

2 Adele Berlin, *The Dynamics of Biblical Hebrew Parallelism* (Bloomington, Ind.: Indiana University Press, 1985), 2.

3 Tremper Longman III, *How to Read the Psalms* (Downers Grove, Ill.: Inter-Varsity Press, 1988), 95.

4 If you know the basics of Hebrew and wish to learn more about grammatical parallelism, you can read Berlin, *Dynamics*.

5 Leland Ryken, *How to Read the Bible As Literature* (Grand Rapids: Zondervan, 1984), 89.

6 Quoted in Tremper Longman III, "Biblical Poetry," in *A Complete Literary Guide to the Bible*, ed. Leland Ryken and Tremper Longman III (Grand Rapids: Zondervan, 1993), 84.

7 Ryken, *How to Read the Bible As Literature*, 90.

8 See John Beekman and John Callow, *Translating the Word of God* (Grand Rapids: Zondervan, 1974), 127, and David L. Petersen and Kent Harold Richards, *Interpreting Hebrew Poetry* (Minneapolis: Fortress, 1992), 50.

9 See Othmar Keel, *The Symbolism of the Biblical World: Ancient Near Eastern Iconography and the Book of Psalms* (Winona Lake, Ind.: Eisenbrauns, 1997). Keel's work provides many graphic illustrations of biblical imagery along with explanatory notes. Another helpful tool for probing images is Leland Ryken, James C. Wilhoit, and Tremper Longman III, eds. *Dictionary of Biblical Imagery* (Downers Grove, Ill.: InterVarsity Press, 1998).

10 For a full discussion of gate as an image see *Dictionary of Biblical Imagery*, 321.

Chapter 3: The Abundant Life: The Psalms as Instruction (Part 1)

1 The New International Version uses the word *destroyed* here, but the Hebrew text uses the same word in Pss. 1:6 and 2:12; see the New American Standard Bible.

2 The New International Version routinely translates this use of *barak* with "praise."

3 This is why the New International Version translates the word for "perish" as "come to nothing" in Ps. 112:10.

4 Ordinary winds are in view in this image, not the winds of tornadoes or hurricanes.

5 See David J. A. Clines, *The Dictionary of Classical Hebrew*, 4 vols. (Sheffield: Sheffield Academic Press, 1998), 1:437, and Ludwig Koehler and Walter Baumgartner, *The Hebrew and Aramaic Lexicon of the Old Testament*, 5 vols. (Leiden: E. J. Brill, 2000), 1:100.

6 John Calvin, *Commentary on the Book of Psalms*, 3 vols. (Grand Rapids: Baker, 1979), 1:xxxvi–xxxvii.

Chapter 4: The Godly Life: The Psalms as Instruction (Part 2)

1 For a technical discussion of the extent of the "instruction of the LORD," see H. G. M. Williamson, *Ezra, Nehemiah*, Word Biblical Commentary 16 (Waco, Tex.: Word, 1985), xxxvi–xxxix.

2 See also Ps. 119:23–24, 77–78.

Chapter 5: The Lord Reigns: The Psalms of the Kingdom

1 Gen. 7:10–11 refers to the flood waters (*mabbul*) that came down on the earth through the "floodgates of the heavens."

2 Space does not permit a complete demonstration of this point, but study Ps. 8, where the ordinary "man" of verse 4 is a king who rules in verses 5–8.

3 Pss. 77:20; 90:1; 99:6; 103:7; 105:26; 106:16, 23.

4 Some scholars think that at an earlier stage in its development the Book of Psalms may have ended with Ps. 119. In this case "blessed" would have opened and closed the psalms, just as it opens and closes book 1 (see Pss. 1:1; 41:1).

Chapter 6: Blessed Is He Who Comes: The Psalms and the Future

1 Ernst Jenni and Claus Westermann, eds., *Theological Lexicon of the Old Testament*, 3 vols. (Peabody, Mass.: Hendrickson, 1997), 3:1393.

Index of Scripture

Mark D. Futato (M.Div., Westminster Theological Seminary; M.A., Ph.D., Semitic Languages and Literature, The Catholic University of America) is professor of Old Testament at Reformed Theological Seminary, Orlando campus. He previously was associate professor of Old Testament at Westminster Theological Seminary in California.

His in-depth study of the Book of Psalms has spanned over twenty years. During that time he has taught the Psalms both on the seminary level and in church seminars and classes. Mark and his wife, Adele, have known the transforming power of the Psalms in the midst of intense personal struggle.

He has also written a major commentary on the Psalms and was part of a team that translated the Psalms for the *New Living Translation*. In addition, he is also author of *Creation: A Witness to the Wonder of God* and numerous articles on Old Testament studies and the natural world.